European Perspe
on Cultural Policy

C000224706

European Perspectives on Cultural Policy

CULTURAL POLICY REVIEWS
Christopher Gordon

REQUIREMENTS FOR A SUSTAINABLE
CULTURAL POLICY
Simon Mundy

UNESCO PUBLISHING

The authors are responsible for the choice and the presentation
of the facts contained in this book and for the opinions
expressed therein, which are not necessarily those of UNESCO
and do not commit the Organization.

The designations employed and the presentation of material
throughout this publication do not imply the expression of any
opinion whatsoever on the part of UNESCO concerning the
legal status of any country, territory, city or area or of its
authorities, of concerning the delimitation of its frontiers or
boundaries.

Published in 2001 by the United Nations Educational,
Scientific and Cultural Organization,
7 place de Fontenoy, 75352 Paris 07 SP, France
Composed by Didier Pauly, F-75020 Paris
Printed by 4 à 4, Paris

ISBN 92–3–103771–4

Preface

The urgency of bringing culture 'in from the margins' to the heart of policy-making, particularly in the context of development, has led UNESCO to relaunch its activities in the field of cultural policy.

The basic push in this direction was made by the World Commission on Culture and Development. In its report *Our Creative Diversity* (1995), the World Commission devoted a separate chapter to the issue of cultural policies, setting out a number of challenges therein:

When culture is understood as the basis of development . . . the very notion of cultural policy has to be considerably broadened. Any policy for development must be profoundly sensitive to and inspired by culture itself. . . . Defining and applying such a policy means finding factors of cohesion that hold multi-ethnic societies together, by making much better use of the realities and opportunities of pluralism. It implies promoting creativity in politics and governance, in technology, industry and business, in education and in social and community development – as well as in the arts. . . . It implies a thoroughgoing diversification of the notion of cultural heritage in social change. With regard to the natural environment it means building better understanding of the profoundly cultural dimensions of environmental management, creating institutions that give effect to that understanding. Finally . . . it requires new research which pays attention to the hitherto neglected integration of culture, development, and forms of political organization.

These imperatives were confirmed by the Intergovernmental Conference on Cultural Policies for Development organized by UNESCO in Stockholm in 1998. Attended by ministers of culture and senior officials as well as representatives of cultural organizations, agencies, associations, foundations and NGOs from 150 countries, the Action Plan adopted in Stockholm provided a framework and set benchmarks for governmental action in the field of culture for many years to come. The Action Plan enunciated important principles: that 'sustainable development and the flourishing of culture are interdependent'; that 'the dialogue between cultures appears to be one of the fundamental cultural and political challenges for the world today'; that 'cultural policies should aim to create a sense of the nation as a multifaceted community . . . rooted in values that can be shared by all men and women and give access, space and voice to all its members'. The Action Plan also listed broad objectives that states should adopt to apply such principles, for example: to make cultural policy one of the key components of development strategy; to promote creativity and participation in cultural life; to reinforce heritage safeguard policy and practice and to promote cultural industries; to promote cultural and linguistic diversity in and for the information society; and to make more human and financial resources available for cultural development. Finally, the Action Plan recommended concrete measures to attain these objectives.

The Action Plan gave UNESCO itself a mandate to establish a new set of activities on 'cultural policies for development'. A programme of activities was therefore elaborated by the Secretariat in 1998/99 and approved by UNESCO's General Conference. Delegates stressed the potential for UNESCO's work to inform cultural policy-making everywhere, not just in the so-called developing countries. In developing, industrial and post-industrial economies alike the flourishing of culture is a determinant of social integration, political democracy and economic equity. It fosters the sense of trust, partnership and solidarity that are necessary in any society in which people must live and work together. Hence, the programme resolution the General Conference adopted authorizes the Director-General

to promote public policies that recognize the central role of culture in development, including the creation of income-generating activities, by mobilizing and sharing information and new knowledge in this domain, in particular concerning the trade in cultural goods, facilitating the elaboration of innovative policy frameworks and strengthening national and local capacities in the management/administration of cultural institutions; and to develop further inter-agency co-operation with a view to establishing close links between cultural and educational, social, health and development policies.

Both the World Commission and the Stockholm Conference had stressed the importance of defining general principles and methodological guidelines for the formulation and implementation of cultural policy. In carrying out its global 'clearing-house' functions, UNESCO therefore intends to identify and share good practice and innovative thinking in cultural policy-making and implementation.

   We have chosen in the present work to draw on recent European cultural policy experience, since significant progress has been achieved since the mid-1980s under the aegis of the Council of Europe. As we ourselves reflected on the establishment of a new programme with worldwide reach, we made it a point therefore to study the latter's cultural policy review process very carefully.[1] The

1. We are glad to acknowledge here the generous co-operation extended to us for this purpose by the director and staff of the Council of Europe's Cultural Policy and Action Division.

objective of this exercise was to induce cultural partners in the various countries to take stock of their national policies with a view to maintaining or strengthening positive aspects, while at the same time addressing possible shortcomings. It was also an opportunity for the Council of Europe itself to obtain a deeper insight into the cultural problems facing its member states, and identify possible solutions.

In our process of consultation we also turned to the specialists who had contributed to the Council of Europe's cultural policy reviews. One of them was Christopher Gordon, at present chief executive of English Regional Arts Boards, who has worked extensively in the United Kingdom as a manager (and voluntary board member) in a variety of arts organizations, as a local government cultural services official at both district and county levels, and for the Arts Council. He is also Associate Fellow in cultural policy at the University of Warwick, and a governor of the University of Southampton, while chairing the Advisory Board of the Fondazione Fitzcarraldo (based in Turin). He has acted both as an external assessor and independent consultant to the Council of Europe for the cultural policy review process. We asked him for an in-depth analysis of the method adopted by the Council of Europe for its national cultural policy reviews, giving an insight into its strengths and weaknesses, and identifying approaches and processes that could be replicated in other regions of the world. His study was one of the basic working papers used at an international workshop on cultural policies entitled 'Assessing Needs, Devising Tools, Imagining New Methods', which was organized at Gällöfsta, Sweden, with the support of the Swedish National Commission for UNESCO in September 1999. Subsequently, it was published in a special dossier on the workshop which appeared in the *Culturelink Bulletin* (No. 30, April 2000). By reproducing it in the present format, we are glad to share it with an even wider audience.

The second study is by Simon Mundy who has also been a consultant to the Council of Europe, as well as *inter alia* to the European Cultural Foundation, the Ford Foundation and UNESCO. A writer and broadcaster, Simon Mundy was the co-founder and first president of the European Forum for the Arts and Heritage and director of Britain's National Campaign for the Arts. He brings the perspectives of a practising artist and arts activist to bear on the conditions and circumstances that he sees as common to countries in Western Europe, North America and Australasia, and which allow him to explore a set of guiding principles designed 'to govern the pursuit of excellence in cultural policy'. Some of these principles appear to be readily applicable elsewhere, others less so; yet others would require some inventive adaptation to very different constraints and opportunities. It is our conviction, however, that the analysis itself can contribute effectively to the kind of cross-cultural exchange in thinking through and implementing cultural policy that the better governance of all our societies requires.

Division of Cultural Policies, UNESCO

Contents

Some general and methodological reflections on the Council of Europe's programme of reviews in member states (1985–99)

Christopher Gordon

Introduction

TERMS OF REFERENCE

The Council of Europe's national cultural policy review series is part of an ongoing thirty-five-year process to try to conceptualize the field of cultural policy. After careful review at a seminar, held in Stockholm in June 1985, of the specific characteristics of the cultural field and the methods already tested in a variety of countries for public policy evaluation, the CDCC (Council for Cultural Co-operation) agreed to adopt the OECD model, but to adapt it as appropriate. To date, reviews in fourteen countries of Europe have been completed and a further one (in Romania) is currently taking place, concurrently with the 'transversal', more issue-based review programme, which has now also been instituted.

This study discusses some of the most significant lessons from the Council of Europe/CDCC programme of national cultural policy reviews. The purpose is to assist UNESCO to share relevant experience with policy-makers in other world regions, assessing strengths and weaknesses of the European process to date, and identifying approaches and processes that might be usefully and productively replicated or adapted elsewhere. Inevitably, this means that more space will be taken up with discussing the constraints and difficulties of the process rather than its successes. It should therefore be emphasized at the outset that the programme has, on the whole, been extremely successful, and has delivered to the Council of Europe a valuable series of high-quality evaluations (with clear recommendations for subsequent action in the countries concerned) at remarkably low cost. The main costs have been borne by the participating states at a ratio of at least 1:4, it has been calculated. My several roles in relation to the Council of Europe's programme have always been as an external assessor, or independent contractor. The views expressed here are purely personal.

BROAD AIMS OF THE PROGRAMME

The ambitions of the programme were set at a very high level. It is no accident that the first two countries to opt into and complete the process – France and Sweden – were those which probably already had the most coherent relevant data, as well as (rather different) traditions of self-reflection in relation to cultural policy. Broadly speaking, three particular outcomes were hoped for: first, each country that had undergone the process would, as a result, be able to improve its own performance and practice; secondly, other member states through the published documentation and shared debate would have the opportunity to reflect on, and adjust as appropriate, their own practice; and, thirdly, policy-makers, cultural managers and observers/scholars would, as the series of reviews progressed, have access to a valuable bank of comparable data.

It is probably fair to say that while the first and second have had valuable impact, the third has proved much more problematic. The main reason for this is that the duration of the programme has (for reasons that will be discussed below) been more drawn-out than originally envisaged, and, in particular, the collapse of the USSR has had an inevitable, but unforeseen, effect on the programme as a whole.

METHOD OF APPROACH FOR THIS STUDY

This has been based upon a survey of the literature produced in the course of the programme, on numerous discussions with valued international examiner colleagues over the years, and with the officials of the Council of Europe (past and present) who have done so much to ensure the delivery and success of the series. I have also made reference to a small number of important articles by academic researchers which comment usefully and wisely on the difficulties inherent in making international comparisons in the field of cultural policy (see Appendix, page 47). The author is familiar with much of the key documentation produced in the course of the programme to date, and has also had considerable practical experience of the process as an independent examiner (rapporteur on Italy; president of examiners' team on Latvia; rapporteur on final stage debate in the Culture Committee of the Council of Europe for both Sweden and Austria; associate author of the 1997 Comparative Study of the programme).

Origins of the programme

IDENTIFICATION OF THE NEED AND PROCESS ADOPTED

Over at least a thirty-five-year period there has been discussion about the possible international benefits to be derived from conceptualizing and comparing cultural policy within Europe. With the case finally made and adopted by the Council of Europe, a working methodology was derived from the OECD's programme of Education Policy Evaluations. The cultural policy reviews have approximately followed the recommended OECD process with these key stages:

- A background national report prepared by/for the national authorities.
- Investigative visits by international examiners (appointed by Council of Europe).
- An examiners' report produced with recommendations and questions.
- A 'review meeting' between national authorities and examiners (half day incorporated into Culture Committee session in Strasbourg . . . that is, not in the country concerned).

IMPRECISE PARALLELS

It should be borne in mind that education is a statutory area of government service provision (at whichever level), backed up by a lengthy tradition of professional policy consideration and evaluation, taking account of quantifiable and 'measurable' results. By comparison with culture as a field of endeavour therefore, education may be said to be both narrower, and with a much more generally accepted and targeted focus on commonly understood objectives. This means that the actual process in relation to education policy is more easy to organize and manage, as well as leading to perhaps more robust and defensible direct comparisons in standards and achievements across national boundaries. In addition, with reference to the conduct and value of the 'review meeting', the OECD's Education Committee is much smaller, and possibly more directly knowledgeable about its own subject area, than the more diffuse Council of Europe Culture Committee. The latter, given the nature of the Council of Europe as an intergovernmental body, contains a large number of national delegations drawn from the international divisions of ministries of culture or even directly from ministries of foreign affairs. While these officials may have knowledge and experience of cultural diplomacy in a broad sense and of monitoring policy within the European institutions, experience suggests that many are unable to participate fully or effectively in detailed debate concerning cultural policy and practical management issues.

COUNCIL OF EUROPE 'THEMES'

From the outset of the programme, the Cultural Affairs Division of the Council of Europe identified a limited number of broad policy 'themes' for incorporation into the review process. This partly reflected past and continuing work within the Culture Committee, and also represented a sensible attempt to facilitate a common perspective in line with the Council's own high-level objectives at the time. It was expected that national reports would at least include statements about, and some initial analysis of, these issues in addition to any others regarded as particularly important for the country concerned. These 'themes' can be summarized as: (a) decentralization; (b) support for creativity; (c) cultural identity and diversity; (d) access and participation; (e) cultural minorities and fundamental rights; and (f) the creative industries.

One of the fundamental difficulties of the series – and one that sharply differentiates it from the education parallel – is that it is virtually impossible to make any objective assessment of 'cultural needs', let alone one that identifies common standards. The reviews cannot evaluate the cultural life of a given country, but only make some attempt at assessing the effectiveness of the cultural policy of the public authorities. Quite apart from the problems of definition (e.g. of 'national' and 'culture'), we immediately encounter the dilemmas of what can reasonably be included in public policy – much of culture being commercially provided – and the reality that different aspects of cultural policy (whether overtly or by default) are usually located in a variety of different departments of government at national level. In both developed and developing countries, the information society and the global economy are remorselessly reducing the capacity of governments to set and control agendas in the way they once thought possible, and this is directly relevant to culture.

It has sometimes been assumed by outsiders, and also by interlocutors during the review process, that it provides an opportunity for attempting to increase the public resources invested in culture. In actual fact, the emphasis of examiners has increasingly been to focus on the efficiency and effectiveness of policy delivery in the country in question. Consequently, 'value for money' is in many ways seen as more important than absolute sums of money – which may not have any particular significance in themselves.

Definitions and boundaries

CULTURE

Culture, as was noted by Raymond Williams in his important study of cultural expression *Keywords* (1985), is one of the most difficult and complex terms in the English language. In the broader European Union (EU) context, it is also worth observing that following the addition of 'culture' to the Treaty of Rome as a legitimate area of operation (Maastricht, Article 128), there is still no clear agreement between the various institutions – still less between the governments of the member states – concerning boundaries and definitions. The Commission's DG X, which had always had some engagement with the 'cultural industries' as an area of economic activity, has chosen to limit its enhanced post-Maastricht remit to artistic endeavour. The EU's Committee of the Regions (CoR) on the other hand has constantly sought (without much success) to expand this to a more holistic sociological and anthropological definition. Even the most recently published Council of Europe national cultural policy evaluation (*Cultural Policies in Portugal*, October 1998) has in its Introduction two pages of semantic reflection and agonizing over the application of the terms 'culture', 'public cultural policy', 'art' and 'evaluation'. The examiners' team came down on the side of evaluation as embracing the financial dimension, as well as the economic, sociological and environmental 'costs' of political decisions.

CULTURE AS A SUPERMARKET?

Even if questions of definition have not been fully resolved through the programme, the evaluation reports have tended to assume some hierarchy of aesthetic and moral values. This implies acceptance of a pyramid model, with the commercial market forming the broad base, and a comparatively narrow and élitist 'artistic' apex. Inevitably, this model brings with it associations of power, privilege and status. Cultural policy may also subliminally encapsulate ideas of moral and intellectual leadership within any given country or society, but this is very difficult to identify. Common understanding has become much more difficult following the entry of former Communist countries to the programme. 'Culture' as an area of economic protection and political importance has been in decline as statism has declined, but may be absolutely vital to reconstructing national identities and post-Communist value systems. How is this to be squared with embryonic democratic systems, unregulated markets, and often wholesale piracy of copyright materials? Artistic endeavour is, more often than not, treated as if it were just one more product which must take its chance in the commercial market-place. It was pointed out at the 1994 Strasbourg seminar for new entrant countries to the programme by the then Deputy Minister for Culture of the Russian Federation that creating the cultural conditions for the rise of a new democratic 'middle class' was mirrored by a steep decline in measurable standards of cultural literacy across society as a whole as compared with Soviet times. What would this actually 'prove'? Nevertheless, under Communist rule, reading – as an individual rather than communal activity – could be regarded as dangerously antisocial! Great care needs to be taken over the interpretation of indicators as measures of progress, freedom, or enlightenment.

BOUNDARIES AND ANALYSIS

Schuster (1987) has argued cogently for what he terms 'anchored boundaries' if cross-border comparisons are to have any real meaning or validity. This means that it is necessary to take a rather narrow set of definitions (e.g. of arts, libraries, heritage and museums) in order to ensure that like is being compared with like through an agreed matrix listing any particular set of cultural activities and policies. This inevitably has to be a selective and limited process. It also implies that broader-ranging comparisons between countries as a whole can only be very approximate and rather subjective, given the huge range of differences and complexities between systems as a consequence of history and practice. To give a few examples: the division of responsibilities between central, regional and local government; the way recurrent and capital expenditure is treated; how training of professional artists and performers is organized; treatment of professionals through the tax and social security systems; involvement of the private sector in institutions, through sponsorship, trading, service delivery and other professional assistance.

Schuster points out that under the constraints of definitional difficulties, 'the country with the smallest "boundary" implicitly gets to set the terms of the comparison'. Kawashima (1995) in evaluating comparative potential makes a distinction between inclusive, anchored and floating boundaries, in an attempt to define the 'largest common denominator'. However, quite apart from these fundamental methodological difficulties, international cultural comparisons have traditionally been plagued with selective political abuse which ignores meaningful context. Europeans working in the field are increasingly aware of the way in which the United States is used as an alternative benchmark to traditional European methods of financially supporting cultural infrastructure. Under the

Conservative government in the United Kingdom over almost two decades, opera companies and others were told to look to American practice as a model of greater efficiency and effectiveness. Leaving aside qualitative and unadventurous repertoire questions, it was never at the same time accepted by the politicians that the Arts Council's annual grant from taxpayers' revenue to the Royal Opera House (implied to be a sign of its weakness) happened to be a remarkably similar sum to the tax foregone to the US Treasury from personal donations to the New York Metropolitan Opera (implicitly a sign of strength). Crude comparison of cash figures without taking account of the cultural differences, which are the product of history, tradition and practice are, therefore, only of very limited value.

NATIONAL

In the course of designing any future evaluations programme, it is also necessary to take account of the Council of Europe's experience regarding interpretations of 'national'. Almost by definition, it was easier for unitary, centralized states to opt in, rather than those that are federal, or have developed more devolved or 'voluntary' (third sector) systems. There can be no doubt that the original ambitious intentions of the CDCC for the cumulative effects of the series have been frustrated through the non-participation of some major European countries which have important messages and examples of good practice to communicate more widely. In particular, Germany, Spain and the United Kingdom are missing. The explanations are different in each case, but worth noting.

Given the strength of the German Länder, it was unlikely that the Federal Republic would be able to see its way to participating. Nevertheless, with its strong traditions and impressive number of important institutions, Germany is a major cultural powerhouse in Europe. But the problems – both political and technical – would be just too great. The same is true of Belgium, where the cultural and political differences between the three autonomous communities argue against the possibility of co-operating with the programme on the terms originally devised. Austria is the only federal state to have entered the programme, and found the experience difficult and quite bruising. The Spanish Government agreed to participate, but had to withdraw embarrassingly after the internal arguments with the regional governments over leadership and methodology could not be resolved. The British Government for most of the period in question was infected with terminal Europhobia, but given the highly developed 'arms-length' cultural policy and delivery systems in place, would in any case have had enormous difficulty in participating. Nevertheless, this model, together with certain more 'business-like' practices derived in part from the United States and the United Kingdom's private sector, could and should have been communicated with advantage to the rest of Europe.

CAN 'NATIONAL' BE SUFFICIENTLY INCLUSIVE?

The focus and route for the programme, at least as conducted in unitary states, is central government. There is, naturally, also a requirement that other levels of government, institutions and the cultural sector (including individual artists) are included in the process as part of building up as complete a picture as possible. There are two inherent problems in this. First, in large countries, the complexities may make this rather difficult to achieve. Second, civil servants can often be too beholden to their political masters, or else defensive of their own unquestioned or unassailable departmental record and practices. Italy is a case in point. The contact point for the review was the Ministry of Foreign Affairs, but a large number of government departments have a role in cultural policy and delivery – and two in particular. Partly because of rivalry between them, the decision was taken to commission the national report from a reputable independent research organization, but one with no particular track record in the cultural field. (It is also worth recording that the most reputable Italian cultural research institutes at the time were associated with the political left, which raised further questions for the government.) Furthermore, the desire of the two largest players at the time (the Ministry of Cultural Heritage and the Department of Performing Arts – situated in the Prime Minister's office) to represent their own highly centralized interests, risked underplaying the equally crucial regional and local authority roles in cultural policy. Nevertheless, the importance of the process itself as a learning mechanism for the national participants should not be underestimated.

National reports and data

PREPARATION AS LEARNING
The lessons to be drawn from the preparation of the national reports in the first six Western European countries are well summarized in John Myerscough's *Comparative Study* (Myerscough et al., 1997, 2.6 et seq.). France and Sweden having been the two states most able to comply with the aims and objectives of the programme, as well as with its evolving

methodology, were also the only two able to draw up their national report within the government administration. This immediately highlights one of the most significant questions concerning the national report: who, and what, is it for? Is it primarily for the public systems in the country concerned, or is it mainly the starting point for the external examiners? To what extent does it have a focused purpose as a vehicle for public debate and comment? If this is foreseen, might it have a damaging effect in so far as those engaged in drafting it feel obliged to consider the public-relations effects, rather than concentrate on presenting the picture as honestly as possible? Where do artists and the audience fit into this? There is no single, or simple, answer to these questions, and the balance between them has inevitably varied from case to case. In a programme of this kind, governments are bound to wish to present their own systems internationally in the best possible light. Consequently, there is always a certain tension between the purely evaluative and the political dimensions of the work.

In the light of developments in society and technology, particularly over the past twenty years, there is a growing gulf between the accepted 'cultural institutions', how they are perceived and underwritten, and how the population as a whole actually 'consumes' its culture. In Western Europe also, the postwar growth of multicultural societies in many cases challenges traditionally unquestioned notions in cultural practice of what is 'professional' and 'amateur', together with demands that public systems adapt in order to allow for equality of treatment over access to public subsidy at a time when, economically, the public sector is increasingly constrained. Any evaluation of a country's cultural policy that focuses almost exclusively on the publicly funded and delivered systems is bound, therefore, to be increasingly patchy and misleading in relation to the cultural life of the country as a whole.

The national report needs to have a number of different functions, which can be successfully combined. It should be a position statement covering values and practice, which should make it an ideal vehicle for informed public debate within the country concerned. It should also provide the springboard for the evaluation by the external team of examiners. Too much detail, too many statistics, too thorough an enumeration of laws is generally unhelpful. Some intellectual rigour is clearly called for, but it should not primarily be a 'researcher's' document. If the process is perceived as researcher talking in technicalities to researcher, or ambassadors to nobody in particular, then it will have little, if any, useful purpose.

METHODS OF PREPARATION

It is instructive to recall the variety of ways in which national reports have been drawn up for the programme:

In *France* the compiler was a senior adviser to the National Audit Office. This was a deliberate choice to involve a senior official who had great knowledge about the sector, but who was free of partiality in relation to particular vested interests.

In *Sweden* it was compiled by a working party in the ministry, but making use of draft material prepared by the National Council for Cultural Affairs.

Austria had already identified the need to build a reputable national research capability, and therefore engaged an independent researcher to establish a totally new organization to provide back-up.

In *Finland*, on a specific political time-scale, the minister aimed for an independent survey of cultural policy. Researchers who were unconnected with the ministry were employed to produce the report under the aegis of the Arts Council's existing Research Division.

In *Italy*, through the co-ordinating Ministry of Foreign Affairs, an internationally well-known Italian research institute (Censis) was commissioned. Censis's reputation largely rests on high-quality work in social, demographic and tourism research, but not in culture.

The Netherlands employed independent researchers to prepare the draft text, besides obtaining significant contributions from the Social and Cultural Planning Office. The government did formally adopt the text.

Portugal entrusted the task to a group of sociologists from the Observatory on Cultural Activities. This organization was founded jointly by the Ministry of Culture, Lisbon University's Institute of Social Sciences, and the National Statistical Institute.

The other completed exercises in the programme have all been in former Communist countries (Estonia, Slovenia, Russian Federation, Bulgaria, Lithuania, Latvia and Croatia). With the exception of the Russian Federation, these are all comparatively small states, and ones in which the enforced historical legacy has had a profound impact on the 'mindset' of cultural policy-makers, administrators, managers and artists alike. The context in every case has required engagement with a profound shift in the perceived function of culture, where state control used to be paramount. Inevitably, with the primary focus of the task here being to devise strategies for the short-term survival and

strengthening of culture under totally new market conditions, alongside institutional impoverishment or collapse, the approach has been more specifically geared to problem-solving. The changed role of culture from 'gatekeeper' to enabler and creator of new opportunities is a massive shift, taking place against a very unstable economic and social background. It is no coincidence that the profile given to the immediate concerns of individual artists (who were often key figures in the struggle for political liberation) in these reviews is much more immediate than in the remainder of the group in Western Europe. The practice has continued whereby governments commission 'independent' researchers to provide a draft national report in consultation with the relevant government ministries, which describes the rapidly changing political, social, economic and cultural background against which the evaluation takes place. In the case of Latvia, a fascinating, and opinionated, introductory essay was commissioned from the country's most noted living writer and poet.

STRUCTURE AND VALUE OF NATIONAL REPORTS

Cultural policy being very much a manifestation (presumed or actual) of national identity, it is no surprise that the series of national reports shows considerable diversity in approach and structure. In order to try to ensure maximum comparability in the original spirit of the programme, the Council of Europe commissioned two detailed and helpful methodological papers for participating countries – one entitled *Guidelines for the Preparation of National Reports*, the other *Cultural Indicators: A Few Examples* (see Appendix page 48). In general it seems fair to say that some of the good intentions have not come fully to fruition for two main reasons. First of all, the Council of Europe's matrix of core themes has not been equally respected or treated by participating countries, which makes direct comparison much harder. Secondly, the expected degree of open self-evaluation has not materialized in most cases. Given the degree of international exposure these exercises involve, public relations and *amour propre* can have a distorting effect, which ultimately reduces the value of the programme's comparative purpose. In the cases where the examiners' reports have had challenging recommendations to make, these can evoke an unhelpfully defensive, or even aggressive, response.

POSITIVE SUCCESSES

Taken as a group, the national reports represent a remarkably positive achievement. We must remember that their production was a rapid learning process for most of those involved. Despite the considerable differences, which are only to be expected, they do present a more coherent picture than the old (albeit still often illuminating) UNESCO series of individual country profiles. It is worth highlighting the following particularly positive points.

In every single case, relevant material was brought together for the first time. This in itself has proved valuable for the individual countries and for constructive debate about the changing context and climate of operation which is universal.

Partly following the example of the excellent Swedish model, the scope of the national reports has been extremely wide-ranging. They are in most cases rather impressive stand-alone documents, which have begun to make an impact on international scholarship, and have led to more challenging thinking on the part of policy-makers. (They are, for instance, much more 'weighty' in both size and substance than the normal background papers produced for the Education Policy Reviews in the OECD prototype.)

The reviews in former Communist countries have been approached with a measure of seriousness and immediacy which demonstrates that, despite the massive public financial problems, the exercises have been timely. They are also often regarded as important contributions to the public debates about cultural identity, the rights of majorities and minorities, and the value systems underpinning the development of civil society.

DIFFICULTIES INHERENT IN THE PROCESS

On the debit side, there are also lessons to be learned. Many of these are constants, which may not be capable of easy resolution, but will nevertheless be relevant to any similar future programme of evaluation. Lack of clear, broadly 'anchored' definitions has continued to create problems throughout the conduct of the series. The balance between the interests of central, regional and local administrations – let alone of the cultural sector itself and the general public – can be difficult to maintain. A 'national' process can have the effect of underrepresenting the role and importance of the other players, even in systems that operate on a federal or devolved model.

The tension between a neutral research-based approach, and an understandable national wish always to put the best foot forward is endemic to the nature of the programme.

The growing bulk of the national reports has in certain cases led to some impenetrability, and the failure to face up to dispassionate self-evaluation or engage with core themes has been limiting.

Reports that are too theoretical, purely research-based or simply catalogue legislation etc. can be rather divorced from the political and social realities with which examiners have to contend.

Timing is extremely important. In a number of instances, the national report was not produced by the date set for it to be available to the examiners as they started on their work. This made the examiners' task more difficult, and is unsatisfactory in relation to the review meeting.

STATUS OF THE NATIONAL REPORT

This, in addition to the question of delivery on time, is a fundamentally important issue for the independent examiners appointed to undertake the detailed review. The range of interlocutors and interests with which examiners have to engage in the course of their investigations is necessarily very large and diverse. Their task is made much more difficult if there is doubt over the status or clearly accepted ownership of the national report. Wangermée (1993, p. 8) observes in relation to national reports that 'preparation cannot be the *exclusive* [my italics] responsibility of a research team'. There is an irony in that while the general feeling around the programme seems to be that independent production is probably a strength, this also allows politicians and officials more space to distance themselves from findings or trends with which they may be uncomfortable. In the case of France, the national report was formally adopted by the minister, thus providing a very secure starting point for the examiners. The Italian report only existed as a changeable draft throughout the course of the actual evaluation, as central government officials in differing government departments constantly tried to influence its final shape to their own advantage, even after the examiners' report existed in draft. The issue of ownership, as has already been mentioned, was the hurdle that defeated Spain's intention to participate at all. The timing of the exercise in Finland was largely politically determined, and there was a clear undercurrent that officials regarded the report as the minister's, and not the ministry's document. The Austrian Länder refused to accept that their 'national' report had any higher status than that of an independent commentary. In the case of Austria, as well as Italy, the Russian Federation, Latvia and Lithuania, changes of minister (in some cases more than once) in mid-process threw it off course.

Independent examination

COMPOSITION OF TEAMS

The Council of Europe has been rather well served by the quality and dedication of its examination teams, within which it secured an impressive degree of excellent and creative thinking at remarkably low cost to itself. Certainly the balance and range of experience and expertise included within the various review teams worked to the advantage of the process. It should be noted in passing that, owing to time-scale difficulties over the production and official agreement over publication of certain national reports, the team appointed by the Council of Europe might occasionally have been further enhanced by the inclusion of particular expertise – but this became apparent too late in the process. The 'themes' established by the Culture Committee did not always produce the optimum 'fit' with the topics seen by some countries as the ones of most immediate importance to them. Consequently, some of the examiners' deliberations might have been strengthened by including, for example, specific expertise in heritage, museums or broadcasting and media.

Selection of examiners, generally a team of four or five individuals, has normally been dealt with by the Council of Europe's Secretariat. The key appointments are the president/chair and the rapporteur (with the latter being paid a modest honorarium under contract for what is a very substantial piece of work). These two may have some influence in the selection of the remainder of their own particular team. Each team is, to whatever extent is possible, a balance of expertise and professional background, country of origin, gender, etc. For the Latvian evaluation, a rapporteur from another former Communist country (Poland) in the same region was deliberately selected. This provided some reassurance to the Latvians themselves, as well as assisting the other four (Western European) examiners greatly in their understanding and interpretation of evidence and comment. When the opportunity has been taken to include a practising artist in the team, additional insights have often been gained. There only seems to be one instance of a team having been knocked off course by becoming more involved in intervening in a live current issue within the review country. These groups, often working in difficult circumstances and under considerable time pressures, tend to develop quite strong and positive group dynamics. A very large measure of responsibility rests with the rapporteur, who is responsible for delivering the team's agreed report. Invariably, the majority of the drafting and further research falls to the rapporteur, after the team as a whole has agreed upon a basic structure and format. It has become the practice within evaluations for each examiner to 'specialize' in pursuing particular themes or topics with interlocutors. The OECD education report process usually farms out a share of the total reporting task (i.e. including the written report) to all the individual team members.

EXAMINERS' FACT-FINDING VISITS

The methodology has been in place *ab initio* for examiners to divide time between engagement in capital cities with ministries, national institutions, etc., as well as with local and regional authorities and other important partners elsewhere in the country under consideration. Serious attempts are made to interview artists so that as comprehensive an overview as possible can be taken. The effectiveness of the visits (usually lasting for only two, at most three, weeks) is very much dependent on the quality of briefing from the key contact point in the review country. This can be variable, but there have been outstandingly good examples. Choice of regional visits, under the time constraints, is extremely important. This is particularly so in large countries, so that the examiners are confident that what they are encountering is relevant, representative of the country as a whole, and likely to illuminate particular aspects of cultural policy productively. This can, of course, be difficult to predict where variety, or sheer size – of country and problems – is a major factor (e.g. the Russian Federation), or where federal or regional differences are very significant (e.g. Austria and Italy). There has been the occasional example of a ministry showing its reluctance and initial resistance to an examining team's considered choice(s) of location, but that in itself can be rather illuminating. Where the team has a particular wish to visit, but the ministry (or central agency) has no contacts, this has usually been successfully achieved through Council of Europe contacts, or other professional networks to which the examiners may have personal access. The number and range of different witnesses and representatives of authority at the various levels who have been interviewed in each case is very impressive.

VALUE OF VISITS FOR THE PROCESS

Since the credibility of the programme rests on an assumption of 'peer review', an important feature is the exchange and discussion of professional experience between the examiners, on the one hand, and policy-makers, artists and managers of companies and cultural institutions, on the other. An additional benefit of the process may be that the sharing of problems previously regarded as local (or indeed national) may lead to their being seen in a common broader, or international, context and therefore more soluble by reference to the experience of others elsewhere. In addition, regional visits can give increased status to culture, and demonstrate the importance of culture being seen holistically as a social and economic force. Interlocutors in the review country often also use the examiners' visits, and key moments of the process, to profile themselves and current issues in the press and media. This in turn has undoubtedly raised the Council of Europe's profile, and added a European dimension into the local and regional cultural policy debate.

SHARED BENEFITS

Since the programme has covered quite a substantial time-scale, and the addition of former Communist countries after 1990 greatly increased its scope, the series of examiners' reports offers a wide and informed insight into cultural policy, its delivery, management and development in Europe over a fifteen-year period. Although it is true that the primary benefit of reviews has been within the country concerned, there is additional benefit for other countries and for students of cultural policy in the availability of comparative material. This is not always data-based, but some of the lessons in published reports have, on occasion, encouraged others to improve their own practice in this very area. Core 'themes' devised for the programme in the early 1980s have been, in some cases, rapidly overtaken by other developments, and immediate crises. A useful appendix in Myerscough's *Comparative Study* (Myerscough et al., 1997) analyses and quantifies the 'read across' from all those reviews to have been completed by that date. Publication and dissemination of the national report, the examiners' report and the note of the review meeting enables a wider community of interest to engage with the material. It is expected that the review country – where the official language is not English or French (the 'official' Council of Europe languages) – will publish the documentation in its own language, and publicize and disseminate the results. Practically all participant countries seem to have done this.

COMPARATORS AND INDICATORS

At the start of the programme, one of the stated objectives was to improve skills and practice in measurement, and to develop meaningful 'cultural indicators'. Examiners have sought to address this, including figures for certain aspects of policy where they have felt this was relevant and of good enough quality. The approach to this has been gradualist, especially since the need for data in evaluations arises out of policy concerns, and not out of theoretical interest. One developing area here has been income ratios – public, private and earned. Most teams have been conscious that any such figures, while useful as benchmarks, need to be used with caution, and only within the particular context and in relation to defined policy discussions. Cultural policy literature generally has too many poor and misleading examples of crude public expenditure as a measure. This is, in any case, controversial as a research tool, as it often proves inaccurate or misleading. Per capita public expenditure is possibly the most powerful summary figure for cross-border comparison, distilling as it does a multidimensional problem into a single, easily understood, measure. Nevertheless, there is a serious danger that indices developed from this confuse, or certainly do not illuminate, breadth of spending with depth. The relevant public expenditure expressed as a proportion of gross national product (GNP) is another valid indicator of the commitment of the public authorities. In terms of research methodology to track policy meaningfully, it is probably most helpful to follow something like this sequence: (a) identify the key issues; (b) set policy objectives; (c) specify measures to achieve objectives; (d) measure results/impact; and (e) evaluate and gauge 'efficiency'.

This will allow for some evaluation of activity which is sufficiently sensitive to context while also taking account of 'inputs' and 'outputs' which should include intangible benefits not susceptible of numerical measurement. Independent work is currently being done in the United Kingdom, but taking account of examples in industrially developed countries across the world, to try to devise a series of 'social value' indicators.

Sensitivity analysis

WIDE PROGRAMME FOCUS

Definitions and boundaries are, we have seen, a major area of difficulty for the programme. Furthermore, despite the Culture Committee having agreed on particular themes which it wished to see dealt with in each and every case, and officials of the Council of Europe having made strenuous attempts to encourage compliance, they do not have the authority or power to insist upon it. There have been examples in which a particular country chooses to ignore some of these themes, since there may be such an overridingly compelling area of interest that is unique to the value of its own participation. Italy's wish to focus on heritage is a case in point, which meant that there was very little possibility during the review of devoting any serious attention to participation of minorities. Given that the process is rather heavy, the time-scale extended, and the costs borne by the state concerned very considerable, it is inevitable that there will be a strong desire to concentrate on those issues that the country concerned considers are most immediate to its needs.

POLITICAL AND DEVELOPMENTAL CONSIDERATIONS

National sensitivities can, as has been observed, be important given the context of the review process (cf. Spain, Austria, Italy). The potential quantum leap in this regard from former Soviet republics has been fascinating, given that there is so much at stake. However, it is remarkable to note the high degree of openness displayed by all those countries to have entered the programme, since the desire to learn rapidly has generally been

awarded much greater priority than to defend the legacy of
discredited systems or policies. Nevertheless, confronting some of
the very difficult and painful truths can be quite threatening –
especially when exposed to the full public process. Representative
examples of this might be Bulgaria (with reference to the
inherited 'mindset' from Communist times) or Latvia's perfectly
understandable hesitancy in dealing with its proportionally
massive Russian 'minority', which has hugely important cultural,
social and political implications. All the Central/Eastern
European countries are to be commended for the rather brave and
open attitudes they have brought to the evaluation programme.

PRAGMATISM VERSUS NEUTRAL RESEARCH

It comes as no surprise that former Communist countries have
wished to make use of the programme more as 'action research' to
help them deal with apparently insoluble problems of
infrastructure, society and their embryonic market economies,
than as a 'comparative' exercise. Specific and individual culture –
and cultural identity, it goes without saying – are rightly perceived
as having played a crucial part in the retention of some dignity
and hope for individuals under the Communist system, and in
the reconstruction of the state as a political entity. Nevertheless,
as a group, these countries have certainly found peer-group
comparison useful at least at the anecdotal level. The original
purpose of the programme did not, of course, envisage the need
for this degree of sensitivity to difficult circumstances, seeing the
objectives more in terms of policy and managerial practice.
Robert Wangermée's *Guidelines*, while asking for rigour in the
treatment of data, stated: 'The Council of Europe would like the
evaluation to be as comprehensive as possible for the task of

maximum comparability between member countries. It is aware, however, that variants may be introduced to take account of the individual situations of the various countries.' (Wangermée, 1993, p. 34.) The Council of Europe's current programme of lateral and thematic reviews is a logical, helpful and intelligent attempt to respond to those sorts of demands from new democracies in particular, but methodologically has set an even greater challenge.

The review meeting

OBJECTIVES AND ADJUSTED PRACTICE

As employed within the Council of Europe programme, there seem to have been three different, but parallel, purposes which can be identified as: (a) marking the formal conclusion of the process so far as the Culture Committee is concerned; (b) offering a platform to the minister and senior representatives from the country involved and (c) opening up the possibility of wider debate, and disseminating good, and novel, practice.

The procedures adopted for these meetings have been varied as the programme has evolved. Originally scheduled for a full day (in two three-hour sessions), practice of late has been to contain the exercise within half a day, sometimes with two evaluations concluded on the same day. In most cases, the relevant (or most appropriate) minister has appeared, backed up by senior officials and key researchers who have been involved in drawing up the national report. The usual practice was for the president of the Culture Committee to chair the review meeting, but latterly this has been changed in favour of the president of the examiners' group (or the rapporteur, if language is a material factor), in order to focus debate more sharply. While this has probably led to some improvement in the productive use of available time, it has also tended to compound the already vexed issue of protocol. Ministers are closely questioned in public not by their peers, but by the examiners, who are mostly independent 'experts' or officials.

RECORDING PROCEEDINGS

Questions, answers and general discussion at the review meeting are recorded, with a summary being incorporated into the published documentation. This summary has normally been produced by an independent rapporteur who has taken no part in the process in relation to the particular country under review. There seems to be general acceptance that this summary adds value and interest for the general reader. The exception to this practice was France (the first exercise completed) where the edited summary of the final session is included in the published report at the conclusion of each relevant section of the document. This is possibly logical and helpful to students or subsequent readers, but loses any real sense of the occasion as a living process. In the case of the Netherlands, the minister did not attend. Ministry officials had prepared rather formal and detailed responses to the examiners' previously submitted list of key questions. This came across as rather defensive, and created considerable tension during the actual meeting, since the examiners naturally wished to have a creative role in open debate, and to keep the proceedings lively for the committee as a whole. In the end, both the formal, carefully worded, written answers, and a précis of such discussion as was possible, were included in the published report. Council of Europe officials believe that in more recent reviews in post-Communist countries, prepared formal responses have proved quite helpful to the process.

BENEFITS OF THE REVIEW MEETING

The review meeting may be said to contribute positively to the whole process in a number of ways.

First, active ministerial involvement underlines the value that participating member countries ascribe to the process. This also suggests that the key lessons learned should go beyond mere defensive tactics on the part of officials, since there is an additional pragmatic political perspective. It also helps guard against any risk that the discussion could become rather too abstract and academic.

Second, the occasion allows for clarification of issues, and expression of any significant differences of opinion or analysis, as well as some updating on current policy initiatives or reforms that may go some way to meeting findings expressed in the examiners' report. This has been particularly important in the case of former Communist countries, where the context is constantly and rapidly shifting.

Third, the meeting, at least in theory, enables other national delegations to take a view on the evidence and conclusions set out in the two key documents. They are able to participate in the general debate and to develop particular themes of interest to them through questioning and making observations.

On the whole, the first two points have been well satisfied, despite the protocol issue discussed earlier. Achieving lively, but reasonably focused, wider debate has been more difficult. The actual composition, and degree of detailed expertise held by members of the national delegations to the culture committee is an issue here. But the key problem is perhaps the very size of the committee. As observed by Myerscough (1997, 3.5), 'The Culture Committee is more like a medium-sized conference than a working committee, and is difficult to manage into active debate'. The sessions have tended to have two particular characteristics. First, they are very heavily weighted towards being a dialogue between the examiners and a minister or ministerial team. Second, comment from committee members is often ad hoc, derived from rather narrow self-interest. It is particularly difficult for the chair of the meeting to run an open, but 'thematically' intelligent and coherent discussion which both involves and develops. Some attempt has been made to tackle this problem through the examiners' producing and circulating in advance a list of key questions arising out of their conclusions. Nevertheless, this has dangers – as we saw in the case of the Netherlands – and committee members may arrive at the meeting without having really engaged properly with the topic, so that the chair of the session has little or no idea in advance what issues may be of general interest, and in what order (or groups) they may be raised in order to manage a lively and productive discussion.

OECD COMPARISON

The half-day now allocated to the review meeting corresponds to OECD's traditional practice. Given the tighter focus on agreed objectives within what is certainly a narrower field, it is no doubt easier to assemble an appropriate collection of senior officials, institutional directors, etc. It is certainly true that the OECD review meetings involve far fewer people which, amongst other things, makes it cost-effective to hold the session in the country concerned. This would have had considerable financial and intergovernmental implications, had the Council of Europe pursued it as a viable alternative to their adopted practice. The Culture Committee has little clout as such, and certainly the national government officials involved do not have the authority to insist upon common formats or data, which would assist the 'comparative' objective.

Outcomes and follow-up

SPECIFIC OUTCOMES FOR REVIEW COUNTRIES

The 1997 review of the programme demonstrated that many of the original aims had been successfully achieved. Analysis of the documentation on individual countries, and the record of internal follow-up sessions (sometimes still involving the Council of Europe – particularly now in former Communist countries, where travel costs for outside 'experts' has often been met) showed that progress had been made in relation to the aims. The area of lesser achievement is in formal comparison of experiences between countries, but this is probably of lesser importance to UNESCO, which is more likely to focus on high-quality 'action research'. Such development of instruments of measurement as there is to show, tends to have been focused upon the immediate policy requirements of those countries in isolation. But, as is observed in the UNESCO *World Culture Report* (1998), 'Many relevant cultural concerns are not reflected adequately through existing statistics' and 'What the indicators do is to present those aspects of world culture that are readily measurable'. This tends to produce an automatic bias in favour of richer countries where there is a pattern of production and consumption of cultural goods which are priced in a market. There is the further liberal economic dilemma that, at least in Western countries, the public cultural policy systems all tend to support from universal taxation the cultural forms most patronized by the higher educated and wealthier social élite, whereas the rest of the population consumes its culture almost exclusively within the context of the market economy. (The political response to this is to tend to stress the need for more widespread or universal education programmes to broaden access and understanding, but this is not in itself a wholly convincing answer.) It seems to be generally agreed that producing high-level cultural development indices is impossible, and probably dangerously misleading.

SOME COMMENTS ON FOLLOW-UP
The Council of Europe analysis (Myerscough, 1997) does detail the individual histories of follow-up and usage of the review documents in the first six (Western) countries to complete the process. The record has been variable, but the positive influence of the actual process can be 'subliminal', and take some time to have a real effect. It is also, of course, often impossible to be precise about cause and effect. Evaluations may highlight some necessary reform, say, which might have taken place anyway, but still could have had a catalytic effect on the timing or detail. In the former Communist countries that have participated in the process, however, this type of challenge has had much more immediacy, not least since many of the key 'objectives' are still in the process of being discussed and politically accepted. Their national reports have often had to concentrate on describing and

attempting to evaluate a very transitional situation, whilst the assessment has gone on within a rather unstable context. The external examiners have therefore frequently found it unproductive to attempt to make actual cultural -policy assessments, but have concentrated instead on policy planning, and resource issues within a context of re-emerging market economies, and civil society. Much of this is about the need to make hard choices in relation to maintaining a viable infrastructure within very weak and volatile public finances, whereas the mental 'conditioning' can still delude people into looking back (nostalgically in one sense) to the times when provision was universal, and the state assumed total responsibility for the cost implications. The exercise in Finland, it should also be noted in passing, took place in rather difficult circumstances against a background of radical policy questioning in the light of economic downturn and a surge in unemployment immediately following the collapse of the USSR.

BENEFITS AND VULNERABILITIES

The programme as a whole has brought substantial benefits, and increased the profile of the Council of Europe. The political commitment generated has been very impressive as has the quality of input and resourcing. Myerscough (1997) calculated that the cost ratio in favour of the Council of Europe has been approximately 4:1. The process as evolved seems to show that international 'peer review' is sound and dependable, and can be applied to cultural policy in spite of the much greater difficulties (as compared with education) in relation to boundaries and definitions. However, as already remarked, it is important to ensure that the 'peer' process – both ways – is not just, at one extreme, a political or, at the other, an academic exercise. For the evaluation to have real meaning and benefits, the participants need to have relevant first-hand and current responsibility for dealing with policy in this area.

Public assistance takes many forms, and the series of completed reports demonstrate these complexities. Cultural policy and expenditure is rarely, if ever, the preserve of a single central government agency. This is a problem of data collection and analysis even in countries such as France – where in 1990 twenty-five government departments were identified as having some relevant role in addition to the Ministry of Culture. Treatment of particular issues has been uneven – but usually there is a perfectly rational explanation. Many key cultural services, such as libraries and archives, are usually operated at local-government level, but the data provided through national contacts has not always allowed for the quality of analysis that might well be internationally comparable. Sponsorship, donations and 'tax foregone' is statistically an extremely difficult area. Creative industries even more so, but possibly easier to treat than the complex territory of culture in relation to public social agendas, fears of artists with regard to the 'instrumentalisation' of culture (cf. current debates within the European Union with reference to the structural funds) and so on.

Copyright law and implementation is a major issue – particularly in the new democracies in Europe – but its policing in the increasingly technological and global context is exceedingly difficult. Professional training has largely been left to one side as an issue of education, but perhaps needs to be more organically linked. Legal, employment and social-security issues can be very complex and technical, but very different from state to state. Broadcasting is also of crucial importance, and is probably underrepresented in the series (attempts were made by the examiners during the Italian review to make a feature of this, but with Berlusconi as Prime Minister during part of the period concerned, it was felt to be just too 'hot' a political issue to be capable of receiving the required analysis). Much the same could be said of the press, which still has a massive cultural influence in the broadest sense.

Conclusions

OVERVIEW

What, then, are the most important messages to be learned from the Council of Europe's experience over fifteen years or so of grappling with its programme? Overall, that it was a brave and important initiative, but also one of great complexity. The process devised was – with the very best intentions – quite onerous, and this was sensibly and pragmatically modified as the series proceeded and particularly in order to incorporate former Communist countries within the programme when they identified its importance to them at a particular moment. The currently modified 'transversal' or 'thematic' series of European cultural policy reviews being run by the Council of Europe is a logical development, which mirrors what it has been doing for a number of years in other sectors. This is likely to be of much more specific and general value as usable 'action research', making a real contribution to developing systems in a group of volunteer countries going through transition, rather than the earlier (and rather *passé*) proposal argued for by some countries of art-form-based transnational comparisons. The Council of Europe is currently evaluating the book sector but it is too early to draw any lessons. Inevitably, these new programmes will tend to put more of a focus than had been envisaged in the original methodology on the importance of management aspects of delivery, resting on trends and description rather than actual statistics. It is also, of course, a less expensive process to engage in.

The first such thematic study is concerned with 'National Cultural Institutions in Transition', while the second will deal with cultural diversity within the contemporary European context. The 'transition' exercise involves detailed evaluation in six participating countries or regions, Cyprus, Finland, Hungary, Lower Saxony, the Netherlands and Poland. The work (still in progress) is fascinating in that it appears to demonstrate much more correspondence in the common understandings and concerns within Europe than is generally acknowledged, and irrespective of the old/new democracy divide. While there are obviously individual problems and interpretations in the former Soviet bloc territories participating, the broad issues arising out of *désétatisation* and privatization are comparable. These, for example, include:

- Downward fiscal pressures and the need for greater economic self-reliance targets.
- Public/private partnerships, and role of the third sector.
- Issues of governance, and appropriate or reducing roles for ministries.
- Issues of decentralization, affecting central, regional and local authorities.
- Privileged status, protection and linkage to the rest of the sector concerned.

Goals agreed for the study seem to have been largely determined within the boundaries that the participants set for themselves. This keeps a pragmatic focus on the work, with a concentration on inside knowledge and levels of understanding within that context, rather than straying into more prescriptive and normative territory which would probably be more contentious and of less practical use.

THE CHANGING CONTEXT
There are obvious conclusions to be drawn in relation to definitions and boundaries. While it is clearly useful to seek to determine how, within financial constraints, priorities are established and delivered, there is now – following publication of *Our Creative Diversity* and *In from the Margins* – a generally accepted broader social and economic context within which cultural policy is seen to be located. However, despite growing acceptance of notions of 'entitlement', it is extremely difficult to make any convincing objective assessment of cultural 'needs'. The evaluations have necessarily been restricted to cultural policy largely as expressed through the public (and predominantly national) authorities, given that it is not possible seriously to evaluate any given country's 'cultural life'. This effectively means a focus on determining objectives, defining programmes of action, and attempting to measure results. Increasingly, with the universal constraints upon growth in public-sector expenditure, this has led to the incorporation of some general assessment of management and efficiency – though not, one hopes, at the expense of effectiveness. Quality costs money, and there is always a balance to be struck here between the policy objective and its means of delivery. A number of countries, which perhaps have

recognized the overall value of the review programme, have not signed up to it because of their scepticism about its direct relevance to their policy concerns. At different times judgemental criteria in the cultural sphere turn on concepts of 'value' which change, and which certainly cannot be measured against wholly objective and quantifiable categories or measures.

CHECKLIST OF ISSUES

UNESCO has led debate on expanding traditional notions of cultural policy, and the Council of Europe for its part has sought to push out the boundaries, particularly by focusing on individual rights and entitlements. When considering evaluation methodology and workable definitions of the territory, it is worth bearing in mind the following quotation from the summary version of *Our Creative Diversity*:

Most cultural policies are focused upon the arts and heritage. The perspective can be broadened, first by moving away from monolithic notions of 'national culture', accepting diversity in individual choices and group practices. Support to the arts and artists is essential; but equally so is an environment that encourages self-expression and exploration on the part of individuals and communities.

Having firmly established that cultural policies driven by national considerations alone are now generally regarded as suspect, and in any case increasingly unsustainable in view of technological considerations, any policy review process must recognize that it must be flexible enough to give proper representation to the levels of activity and participation to which individuals can relate. It is no accident that within Western Europe the focus

increasingly falls on regions, and above all cities, as the key units
of cultural significance and interest. With these concerns
uppermost, they can be applied to the following summary list of
technical issues arising out of the Council of Europe's
programme:

Clarity of purpose. Who is intended in any future programme to
be the primary beneficiary? The individual country
concerned or the sponsoring organization in relation to its
own profile? The answer to this question will, subject to
certain uniform core design features, determine the degree
of flexibility permitted.

Time-scale envisaged. How many years is the programme to run
for? The answer to this will influence both its pace and the
number of exercises. The Council of Europe process,
having been quite heavy, only allowed for a maximum of
two completions per year, though this speeded up a little
with the reviews of relatively small former Communist
countries.

Comparative purpose. If there is a primary or secondary intention
that the series of evaluations is to have some transnational
comparative function, then there needs to be clear
acceptance by all relevant parties about those areas
concerned, with minimum data standards also agreed and
delivered. The planned duration of the programme as a
whole will have some bearing on the validity of any
comparators accumulated.

National report. It is important that there be a clear process and
time-scale through which there is agreement about its being
ready for release. Failure to deliver on time caused great
problems for the independent examiners in several cases.

However it is produced, there needs to be clear acceptance of ownership by the authorities in the country concerned.

Cost. Given that the process as originally devised is quite onerous, the costs fall quite heavily on the country concerned. While this was not a problem in developed countries, the commitment required of former Soviet-bloc states can seem considerable. This relates mainly to research, writing and production of the national report, and travel, accommodation and all visits/attendances for the examiners within the country. The Council of Europe has covered travel costs from home base to port of entry.

Peer review process. The sponsoring organization in selecting the independent 'peer group' team of examiners should be aware, and mindful, of any particular special areas of concern relevant to the particular country's cultural situation. Sufficient time should be given to this independent team to deliver the quality of work they feel necessary, within the obvious constraints.

Remuneration. Only the rapporteur for the examiners is paid a fee for the time and effort involved (and that at a fairly modest level). Originally the chair of the group received an honorarium, but this practice was discontinued. This tends to reinforce the tendency for the rapporteur to have to shoulder the responsibility disproportionately. The general level of quality among examiners is to some extent a tribute to the perceived value and interest of the exercise, but non-payment must also be a constraint upon choice of involvement.

Examiners' report. This should remain wholly independent, and – as a condition of entry to the programme – should be published and promulgated in the language(s) of the country under review.

Review meeting. This requires rethinking both in terms of size, process and likely efficacy. Consideration should be given to conducting it within the country concerned in order to create wider and more informed public interest in the actual issues. Follow-up debates or seminars in the country concerned, with representatives from the cultural sector present, have proved effective. This has the additional by-product of necessitating translation of the key documents into the indigenous language(s), thereby rendering them more accessible to the press and the public.

Flexibility. The programme, in order to have sufficient coherence, requires a central format which engages a range of defined topics of importance in all cases. However, in order to increase its value above being a purely academic exercise, it needs to have sufficient flexibility and responsiveness to particular issues for the country or region under consideration, whether articulated by it or not.

Follow-up. Without constructive action, following examiners' recommendations/conclusions, and discussion with those politically responsible in the states concerned, the process is reduced to an academic exercise. It is probably therefore helpful for evaluations to feature topics for review which the country itself has identified as being of importance to it at that particular time.

PERSONAL RECOMMENDATIONS

The key messages from the Council of Europe's programme are very positive. For the purpose of UNESCO's consideration, certain adaptations might be appropriate and beneficial. Peer-group evaluation (subject to the 'peers' being appropriately professionally engaged with, and responsible for, policy and its implementation) should be a central feature. The examiners' report should retain its fully independent status. The issue of remuneration might, however, need to be addressed. The time-scale for each successive review should be contained so that it is not allowed to spread and result in unhelpful delays and problems. The production of the 'national' (or equivalent) report should be complete before the external examiners are involved in the process. The national report should be a reasonably rigorous document intellectually, but not be loaded with too much supporting detail. It should also include some self-appraisal and a 'moral/civil' element, as well as encompassing a description of institutional/financial/systems and managerial issues. There might well be some comparative benefit within a broad regional context, but the bulk of the effort should be devoted to problem-solving and constructive progress rather than to comparison as a major objective. There will need to be a clear understanding on the definition of any areas/sectors to be evaluated. 'Participation' proved to be quite a slippery term over the course of the Council of Europe's programme. In UNESCO's much broader context, traditional, informal and community-based cultural forms will presumably assume a much higher degree of importance (by contrast with 'professional' institutions and a market for cultural consumption) which will require some framework of evaluation.

Finally, serious consideration should be given to designing a reduced – but sharply focused – final stage in the particular country or region concerned, which should also involve public debate and media comment. If it were felt to be necessary or desirable, UNESCO could organize occasional parallel debates on regional or themed trends and conclusions for wider interest and consumption.

APPENDIX: DOCUMENTATION AND REFERENCES

General

FEIST, A.; FISHER, R.; GORDON, C.; MORGAN, C.; O'BRIEN, J. 1998. *International Data on Public Spending on the Arts in Eleven Countries*. London, Arts Council of England. (Research Report, 13.)

FEIST, A.; HUTCHISON, R. (eds.). 1990. *Funding the Arts in Seven Western Countries*. London, Policy Studies Institute. (Cultural Trends, 5.)

KAWASHIMA, N. 1995. Comparing Cultural Policy: Towards the Development of Comparative Study. *The European Journal of Cultural Policy*, Vol. 1, No. 2, pp. 289–307.

MYERSCOUGH, J. (ed.). 1984. *Funding the Arts in Europe*. London, Policy Studies Institute.

SCHUSTER, J. M. D. 1987. Making Compromises to Make Comparisons in Cross-national Arts Policy Research. *Journal of Cultural Economics*, Vol. 11, N°. 2, pp. 1–36.

WILLIAMS, R. 1985. *Keywords: A Vocabulary of Culture and Society*. Revised edition. Oxford University Press. 349 pp.

Council of Europe relevant background texts

Diversifying Procedures and Methods to Overcome Perceived Problems. (Culture Committee Secretariat Memorandum, October 1997, CC-Cult, 93:23.)

European Programme of Evaluation of National Cultural Policies. Cultural Indicators: A Few Examples (Augustin Girard) (DECS-Cult., 92:6.)

European Programme of National Cultural Policy Reviews: Experts' Reports – Issues Addressed (1995). (Tabulations.)

European Programme of National Cultural Policy Reviews: National Reports – Issues Addressed (1995). (Tabulations.)

Experimental Programme for the Appraisal of Cultural Policies: France. (DECS, 1987.)

In from the margins: A contribution to the Debate on Culture and Development in Europe. 1997. Council of Europe.

MYERSCOUGH, John; GORDON, Christopher; DUFTON, William. 1997. *European Programme of National, Transversal and Sectoral Cultural Development Policies: Comparative Study.* (DECS-Cult/CP, 97:2.)

Report of Methodology Seminal for New Member Countries. (DECS-Cult/CP, 94:4.)

WANGERMÉE, Robert. 1993. *Guidelines for the Preparation of National Reports.* (DECS-Cult/CP, 93:3.)

COUNCIL OF EUROPE PUBLISHED NATIONAL REPORTS AND EXPERTS' REPORTS

Austria, Bulgaria, Croatia, Estonia, Finland, France, Italy, Latvia, Lithuania, Netherlands, Portugal, Russian Federation, Slovenia, Sweden.

Requirements for a sustainable cultural policy in Western Europe, North America and Australasia

Simon Mundy*

Introduction

This study was commissioned by the Cultural Policies for Development Unit of UNESCO as part of the follow-up to the 1998 Intergovernmental Conference on Cultural Policies for Development held in Stockholm. It covers Western Europe, North America, Australia and New Zealand because, although they have markedly different ways of supporting their culture, the countries of these regions all share roughly the same level and type of cultural infrastructure. They also all face a challenge to this infrastructure from some political parties and from numerous minority groups (some indigenous, some immigrant) who feel alienated by it or feel that their cultural expressions do not have an adequate status in the predominant culture, much of which derives from post-Renaissance Christian Europe. Just as we celebrate the new millennium (on the wrong day, in the wrong

*© Simon Mundy 1999. Certain rights of reproduction, translation and publication held by UNESCO. All rights reserved.

year and as the result of very shaky historical calculations – but such niceties would take too long to explain to those intent on having a good party), it is useful not to be too self-congratulatory and to articulate the guiding principles for the governance of our culture.

While the study covers this wide territory, it only occasionally refers to and does not seek to analyse the policies of individual nations. Such a task would require a far longer piece and is perhaps a function of UNESCO and the respective governments themselves later. Instead I have tried to look at circumstances that are common to all and lay down a series of recommendations to govern the pursuit of excellence in cultural policy. I hope to provoke thought, concentrate a mind or two and offer a checklist against which the basics of performance can be assessed.

This is a challenging period in world politics and social development. Those of us who believe that the values and achievements of our cultures are worth celebrating and taking further have to work hard to make them accessible to all in a democratic society. We need to respect the individual (from whom and for whom the culture is fashioned). We need to pause for a moment in our enthusiasm for valuing technological media and economic results over and above the quality of ideas and discourse. We need also to bequeath to the children of the world a heritage that holds fascination and that they can treasure, together with the means to enjoy it.

The character of policy

Every country has a cultural policy, even if the policy is that there should not be one. This is a reality that has taken shape remarkably recently. It is a by-product of several political and social movements that ran their course in the twentieth century. Nationalism was a driving force, as it had been for much of the nineteenth century. A broad curriculum in education was a spur to the development of a conscious cultural policy and the bureaucratic rationalization of all levels of government spending in civil democracies necessitated it. Culture matters most to people when they feel their way of life and identity is being questioned or is threatened by processes, whether economic, military or political, over which they have (or feel that they have) little control. Consequently cultural policy is most important and carries most status in government when either the country is too small to be a significant economic or military power or when the assumption of power is being challenged by new forces which appear to undermine their historical position. So France and the Netherlands, fearful for the future international usage of the French and Dutch languages, regard a protective audiovisual policy as inseparable from national security. Slovenia, just emerged as a coherent state after centuries of external dominance but without significant resources, has only its culture with which to carve out a distinct existence.

At the other end of the scale the United States of America, disparate racially and geographically but dominant militarily and economically, eschews a formal federal cultural policy except in its upholding of industrial free market rules. Many in the United States see national cultural policy itself as a threat to individual choice and business expansion. It has the size, wealth, power, linguistic security and financial traditions to make the positive articulation of cultural policy a potential admission of weakness rather than the civilized contribution to the lives of its people that other, less formidable, states regard as their duty. Instead it conducts policy mainly at the state and city level, where the emphasis is as much if not more on the leverage of funds from the private and foundation sector than on providing from the public purse.

This chapter is an attempt to look at what ingredients cultural policy in developed economies and mature democracies will need in the coming decades if the expectations and potential of their citizens are to be realized. The countries it covers vary widely in size from isolated islands to continental powers, from cultures that have formed the political reality of the last 400 years to reviving survivors of societies that boast prehistoric roots. It treats as similar Europe, which has almost no border that can be said to have been settled for more than a century, and the vast open spaces of Canada, the United States, Australia and New Zealand, with their feet in a colonial European tradition which has (ironically) found greater stability thousands of kilometres from home.

Europe itself, although it enjoys general acceptance of the need for financial support for cultural activities from public authorities, has widely differing traditions governing how that support is delivered. It varies in generosity, in the range of activity deemed eligible and in the level of government by which it is delivered. There are national, regional and local ministries of culture, arts councils, film boards, public and private broadcasters, overseeing bodies, executive associations, diplomatic promotion agencies, semi-official foundations and lottery funds. There are times when the citizen earning a professional living from culture can be forgiven for feeling that he or she is very far from being the traditional embodiment of the artist, intellectually free and unfettered by corporate structures. Instead the artist has more layers of bureaucracy managing or supervising less public investment than is the burden of any other area of human endeavour.

Culture, the great Welsh writer Raymond Williams once said, is 'one of the two or three most complicated words in the English language'. I would suggest that it is also one of the most inflammatory. It involves so much passion. It contains so much that is central to our freedoms and sense of who we are and where we belong, that it cannot be delivered like health care or taxation. When manipulated with determination it can be an excuse for war. Yet it holds within it the means of reconciliation. Culture can preserve self-respect and be an excuse for ignorant cruelty. It can provide a society with a demonstration of brilliant civilization and show it to be depressingly primitive. It can be treated as the core of our pride, informing every aspect of the imprints we leave to future generations on our patch of world, or it can be the ephemera of societies entertaining themselves with self-conscious trivia. To offer governments a map for sustainable cultural policy is to offer them one that will be covered in contour lines, full of inconvenient road markings and features that will look very different in reality than they do on the two-dimensional plane of the chart.

Perhaps because each country sees its culture as a measure of its distinctiveness – nobody wants to be just like the neighbours or to admit it when they are – the mechanisms for delivering public finance to cultural activity are as individual as the fractured nature of the world would suggest. Broadly speaking, however, the systems fall into three groups: a Franco-German group, an Old Commonwealth and Northern Europe group, and the United States. As in so much of its public affairs, the United States seems to pursue a course largely unrecognizable to those countries that are counted among its natural allies in political, linguistic and religious terms. However, it seems likely, too, that over the next half-century common features will emerge, fed by the scarcity of public funds in Europe, Canada and Australia and by the need for more stability and greater accessibility in American cultural organizations. There is also increasing international pressure for the United States to develop some degree of governmental equivalence so that it can be involved more constructively in intergovernmental discussions, as Germany has recently done.

The Franco-German model is one of state finance directly channelled from government. In Germany, Belgium and Spain the emphasis is on regional and civic authorities, with the federal level playing a relatively minor part. In France, Italy, Turkey, Central Europe, Denmark, Sweden and Norway the central government is the most influential source, with municipalities and regions playing a vigorous but secondary role. The traditions of both reflect the reliance in previous centuries on patronage from the court and city treasuries, with support of culture being seen as a duty of the state just as necessary as defence or diplomacy. Indeed culture was supported as much as an aspect of demonstrable diplomacy as a means of private and public satisfaction.

For various reasons (one of which has probably been the greater role for public as opposed to aristocratic initiatives under a constitutional monarchy) Canada, the United Kingdom, Ireland, the Netherlands, Australia and New Zealand – along with smaller states which take their governmental models from them – have developed a system which places a layer of semi-independent bureaucracy between political control and cultural organizations. Finland, perhaps in order to cut a different path from that of its previous imperial masters, has also adopted a system that distances government a little.

There are advantages and disadvantages in all these approaches. It would be intellectually tidy to invent a system of tax-based support that could be applied to all countries with equal success, flexibility and freedom from political interference. However, nothing could be more unrealistic. All countries are coming to realize that there are in fact few things more political than the presentation and continuance of their culture. There is also a great deal more to it than funding mechanisms. The United States has recognized the problem by trying to remove culture from the list of federal responsibilities altogether with the caveat of a small place for the National Endowment for the Arts and the National Endowment for the Humanities, both funded but frequently attacked by Congress. Indeed every assault by religious, socially puritanical or other congressional interests serves as an example of the reason why the system has traditionally separated the two. The mutual incomprehension is almost total.

None the less, while it is likely that countries will retain their basic systems for the foreseeable future, they are borrowing from each other fund-raising methods, organizational structures and new forums for cross-border co-operation. It is inevitable that good ideas will be shared. The development of the European

Union and its process of associating periphery states, the revival in cultural energy (however temporary) at the Council of Europe, and the informal network of cultural ministers launched in 1998 through the good offices of Canada, all mean that officials are meeting and talking together in a way that has never before happened to such an extent in the government of culture. But there is a limit to how far equivalence can go. This was painfully learned by the army of Western cultural management consultants who invaded Eastern Europe after the collapse of the Soviet Union, each convinced that the model they were bringing from their own country could be slotted neatly into the hole left behind. They were wrong. In fact the means of supporting culture are umbilically linked with the expectations of government in their host countries. They cannot be transferred without risking a disastrous bureaucratic failure and a traumatic seizure in the body of cultural organizations.

All countries need to retain systems that those operating and living within them can understand. They also need reform if they are to meet the expectations of citizens, the challenges of internationalism and the stresses within cultures in a period when the borders drawn on the map tell only a small part of the cultural story.

Emerging policies

Whatever the delivery mechanisms, there are policies gaining fresh importance which have similar elements. These respond to social pressures which, because the economic and political systems are shared, elicit comparable responses. The emphasis placed by each country will fluctuate, of course, but some common ground is clearly visible. As coalitions of states group together to co-ordinate or pool executive power, so the parallel devolution accelerates towards a regional level of decision-making for issues which are less likely to have an international corporate dimension. Culture, which is by nature more easily identified with homogeneous groups than diffuse ones, is seen as one of the main areas for local control. Its economic structures are small scale in the main (with the exception of the broadcasting media), it involves few matters of strategic importance and it is naturally suited to the ambitions of local populations and the politicians who represent them. Nowhere does the American corporate dictum of 'think global, act local' apply more appropriately than in the cultural sector. Consequently those countries like Germany, the United States and Australia, which have traditionally dealt with culture at the regional state level, are reinforcing the commitment (while making belated moves to appoint federal officials able to represent the nation state at international meetings).

Even countries that have been loath to cede authority from the centre, like France and England (used here in its strict geographical sense, leaving out the other components of the United Kingdom) have made significant moves in recent years to transfer executive decisions to personnel based in the regions, even if they still operate under the umbrella of central government. This will lead to the increasing professionalism of regional cultural administrators. It will also necessitate new alliances between them which will not be forced to coincide with traditional nation-state borders. Instead communities of interest are likely to grow up between like-minded local authorities –

those strong in film policy, perhaps, or those with bilingual cultures.

Just as people working in the cultural sector are learning to network in a multifaceted array of service organizations (see below), so regional officials are starting to seek common solutions to shared problems which may be irrelevant at a federal tier. This may happen at first at a fairly superficial level – the formation of a European Network of Cities of Discovery and the co-production of events between Wales, New South Wales and Catalunya are examples from the 1990s – but obvious opportunities for exchange and mutual enterprise will emerge in the coming years. Joint publishing and new technology ventures, the co-production of festivals, common training and education methodologies, are all areas in which the economies of scale most suit medium-size political units rather than those operating as nations (leaving aside the micro-states or those with populations under about 3 million).

Many of these regions also have their language as a reason for wanting to act outside the parameters set by the federal/national level. The world's languages should have flourished in the twentieth century. It was an age of incomparable communication, of massively increased literacy and of access to information. Yet it was also the century when many languages died, assaulted by colonialist insensitivity, the need to travel to find work, the wholesale migration and transportation of populations and sometimes just lack of interest. Often languages were killed off by the last generation to speak them fluently; parents failing to teach their children, feeling that the old language would be a disadvantage in a bright new world where the majority languages of Europe and Asia's imperial powers were all that were needed or safe to know. The dominant powers beat languages out of children, then there was nothing left to learn. Ironically it was those powers that now preach multiculturalism most vehemently – France, the United Kingdom, Spain and the Netherlands – which only fifty years ago, within the working lives of today's pensioned state officials, pursued the most virulent campaigns of minority-language eradication.

Just as the same generation of officials misjudged the importance of biodiversity in the environment, so they failed to understand that linguistic diversity is the depository of human expression. Once we start dealing constantly in the cadences and sentiments of a language that is not our first, the expression is constricted. American English is a case in point. For most of the citizens of the United States, English was learned by a previous generation as immigrant adults. Because of the need to be understood by a population for so many of whom English was a foreign tongue, American English lowered the number of words in usual circulation, borrowed syntax from German (the language of many late nineteenth- and early twentieth-century immigrants) and began to make the few familiar words multi-purpose by compounding phrases, using nouns as verbs, adjectives as adverbs and simplifying the rules for prepositions. It was linguistic rationalization as logical and ruthless as any 'downsizing' (a word that makes the point perfectly) in a General Motors car factory.

The mood is now swinging the other way, and the cultural policy that is emerging is one of rehabilitation of endangered languages, parallel promotion and expanded usage. In the United States and Canada this involves the indigenous American languages, American French and Spanish; in New Zealand,

Maori; in Europe (among many) Basque and Gaelic, Cornish and Slovenian, Alsatian and Faroese. There is, inevitably, a measure of anthropological curatorship about some of the attempts and, rather like those who preserve folk dress and home-cured skins, there is an element of consigning lesser-used languages to a museum culture; curiosities treated with respect, applauded but, in all honesty, not visited very often. But it is at least better than eradication, and gives people of a new generation, anxious to attach themselves to something that reinforces their identity, a chance to rekindle enthusiasm and explore fresh avenues of expression.

Language policy does not just have to include renewed interest in indigenous tongues and dialects, however. In all major countries there is also the need to deal with the expectations of immigrant groups who, whether through the aftermath of colonialism, persecution or economic desperation, have moved to a new home. In some cities in the United Kingdom, immigrant populations are within sight of constituting the majority. In many American communities the source nation of settlement still provides the basic culture. In the Mediterranean the influence of Africa on Southern Europe is becoming just as pervasive as European influence on North Africa. Increasingly the reality of the Mediterranean Sea's true status as a big lake is becoming clear. The policies evolving to deal with this linguistic multiplicity range from bilingual road-signs and official forms to television and radio stations, expanded school curricula and the proliferation of translation booths at conferences and in council chambers.

For most people, defence or championship of a minority language is a gesture of solidarity with a relatively local region, often one downtrodden (then overlooked) by the great imperial states of the last three centuries. There are some notable exceptions, where a substantial language group is put into the position of being a local minority by geographical isolation; for example the French speakers of Canada and Louisiana or the Dutch speakers of the West Indies. For all immigrant groups in Western countries the same issue arises. Turks in Germany, Punjabis in the United Kingdom, Greeks in Australia feel it necessary to make great efforts to retain linguistic loyalty as a sign of cultural inheritance.

The aim of many cultural activities is to cement a group of people together in a common pursuit which establishes their distinctiveness. Sometimes this is inward-looking; the participation of outsiders as other than appreciative spectators is unwelcome. Once the activity seeks out a market, however, the aim changes and it becomes important to reach and be enjoyed by as many people as possible, whatever their own cultural perspective. Once this is allied to the commercial logic of business expansion, it becomes inevitable that an attractive, well-constructed and readily available cultural product will pervade all those areas of other, unrelated, cultures which are susceptible to commercial exploitation. This is globalization. If one is lucky enough to be the producer of culture of global appeal (or merely astute enough to ensure that it has it) then global reach can bring self-confidence as well as riches. Californian film, British television and theatre, French wine, Australian beer, German music and Italian opera have achieved a measure of global success that underpins the world's perception of the country of origin.

For those genres that achieve global ubiquity, the process is self-evidently beneficial. However, for those whose similar genres are worthy but less successful, global competition can seem a disaster, especially as barriers to trade are removed and the traders in globalized products seek to outlaw special help – official promotion or subsidy – which might create rivals. So (to use the same nations to illustrate the issue) Californian theatre, British art music, French film, Australian painting, contemporary German literature and Italian olive-oil production feel as threatened by globalization as the minority cultures have always done by those more dominant around them.

If, however, the sign of cultural success is that its manifestations are available and enjoyed by a wide variety of people across the world, then the aim must not be to restrict global availability but to open it up to the greatest diversity of cultures. Only the most defensive and bigoted cultures make a virtue of their exclusivity. Indeed new means of publication and transmission are making it ever easier for small and regional cultures to find widespread distribution. Welsh film-making, Cherokee web sites, publicity for festivals in Iceland, are becoming accessible with a facility that would have been unthinkable even in the 1970s.

Globalization is an opportunity, but only if the legislative framework recognizes that some cultures and genres will need the sort of financial support which would be unacceptable in commodities governed entirely by free-trade logic. Making cultural activity viable and available is potentially an important element in future peace. If cultures are forced to compete solely on their merit as consumer entertainment products, the rules of domination will create significant resentment. It is too simple for cultural competition to become a mask for nationalistic denigration. There has to be a mix of effective, market-driven promotion and judicious public financial and legislative support. The purpose is not to discriminate against the products of certain cultures (Hollywood film being the example that causes most disagreement) but to act in favour of cultural products and activities that might otherwise find it a struggle to reach beyond a small market and, therefore, if forced to rely on fund-raising purely from the private sector, might not reach a public at all.

Reaching the public, whether local or international, is the goal of all of those professionally engaged in cultural activity. Therefore, access must be at the heart of political strategy. Access for all has become the dominant cultural policy for governments in the United Kingdom, Australia and North America. For the most part this is a matter of recognizing the political reality of who votes democratic governments into power (no longer a small group of wealthy brokers). But it also has a less cynical side, an attempt to broaden the base of modern cultural participation beyond highly educated and prosperous groups and to give those without a tradition of involvement in 'high culture' a sense that their activities are also important. In the German and German-influenced systems of cultural provision, low ticket prices backed by subsidy and the peer pressure of social inclusion have made formal culture an inherent part of civic life for more than 100 years. Simultaneously, though, there is a paradoxical shift away from systematic cultural teaching in state education in many countries which otherwise give a high profile to culture. Music has all but disappeared from many American schools. Fine arts, drama and literature are becoming specialist subjects. In much of Europe, where the arts have had a low profile in the formal curriculum in the past but one that is secure in the daily life of the school, there is a tendency now to regard cultural education as a soft option. Although the demand to be taught arts subjects in universities continues to rise, at school level mathematics, science and main foreign languages are regarded as being more relevant than artistic subjects and smaller languages, despite the weight of evidence showing that these areas are significant contributors to the mental agility, self-confidence and behavioural stability of children.

There is one simple rule (everywhere except the United States) that governs why access has to be an increasingly important aspect of policy. At a time when voters are less and less inclined to accept the case for high direct taxation, governments realize that, if everybody contributes money to cultural services, they will expect that those services are not only available but are seen to reflect the tastes and interests of the majority, while providing minorities (everybody, after all, is part of a minority in some way) with a sense that their interests also have rightful place. In the United States the horror of direct taxation, allied with the tradition of individual philanthropy, has meant that public authorities have a smaller part to play. None the less the foundations, which constitute the corporate reality of American cultural policy, pursue initiatives that are little different from those of Western governments when it comes to directing their own institutions.

Intellectual access also needs to be complemented by physical access and here those governments that traditionally support culture out of taxation are finding themselves in a vice between their philosophical and their financial inclinations. Philosophically they are aware that disadvantaged groups – those with physical disabilities, for example – have ordinary rights but special and expensive needs. Providing the type of universal access to live performance or the built heritage that people have come to expect of public broadcasting or the health system strains the purse strings of government beyond breaking point. Yet the rationing of access is anathema to political parties committed to equality of opportunity and the disparagement of élitism.

Similarly, while the majority of people now live in towns or suburban communities, the countryside holds a reservoir of valuable cultural wealth. Rural areas in the British Isles and Northern Europe also have a higher than average proportion of their population engaged in earning a living through culture, partly out of inclination, partly because of the contraction in other forms of employment and the tendency to reuse important but redundant buildings as cultural resources.

Cultural provision in the countryside is not the same as in the towns, however. Building a theatre, holding concerts and festivals, making sure that there are libraries in small communities, is not enough – though failure to provide or maintain them causes great anger and political trouble. In the country the maintenance of the landscape itself and the traditional practices that stem from it – hunting, sheep-dog trialling, ploughing competitions, grape-picking festivals, the ceremonial preparation of meats and the reverence for the spirits of place – are vital to the cultural health of a civilization. For governments elected by predominantly urban populations, who often regard such rural affairs as at best quaint and at worst barbaric, forging a policy that looks after the totality of culture within their territory is proving difficult. However the confluence of the advocacy movements for environmental and cultural interests is beginning to mean that governments are having to take the stabilization and enhancement of the cultural environment seriously, whether it be rural or urban.

The cultural environment is a useful concept. It embraces the totality of cultural patrimony and activity, and accentuates the parallels with stewardship of the natural world. The term can give a mission to all cultural policy. Stimulating and securing the cultural environment would be an admirable aim for any public servant. The use of cultural activity as a means of development is becoming a vital feature of policies fostering rural regeneration. There are few other forms of work that can replace agriculture as a means of providing a living without aggressively damaging the environment or replacing rural communities with ill-placed urban ones.

It is not only in the countryside, though, that culture is being used for economic and social purposes which themselves have little to do with culture. Whether it be through gradual enlightenment that security, a high standard of living (relative to either the rest of the world or even to 1945) and social mobility do not of themselves bring contentment; or whether it is because politicians have run out of constructive ideas, culture is being cited as the means of delivery for a widening basket of political goods. As heavy industry, agriculture and manufacturing decline – and as the thought of joining bureaucracies or financial service companies as a career loses its charm along with job security – so cultural industries are expected to offer a new way. The arts will provide the creative research and the raw material of talent (the idea runs) while high technology, distribution and management in cultural industries with global markets provide new careers, diverse and dispersed business and personal fulfilment. To this economic benefit, the cultural agent of regeneration will add the balm of social cohesion, career structures which last people well past the traditional age of employment, a meritocracy based on ideas (not rank or wealth) and security built upon respect, tolerance and dignity.

None of this is untrue or bad. The laudable result is that every area of public activity becomes culturally aware. Culture is used to enliven railway trains, spread the awareness of social responsibility, integrate immigrant lifestyles, revive moribund cities and occupy the unemployed or the retired. Yet this process of 'instrumentalization' does value culture for its contribution to the policies of social engineering rather than for itself. There is the danger that culture cannot deliver the benefits ascribed to it in anything like the volume or the time-scale that politicians hope, with results that could prove culturally and socially damaging, as will be discussed below.

The level of cultural industrialization that will be sustainable may be very different from that dreamt of by anxious politicians desperate for new vitality in areas that have become economically redundant. This will certainly be the case unless people are encouraged to use culture actively from an early age. Cutting school investment in books, music and art may have the disastrous effect of limiting the market for cultural goods and services at precisely the moment at which developed economies become dependent on its success. If governments are serious about maintaining a high level of cultural participation which is able to sustain economic activity at a local as well as the global level, then there must be a more determined effort to stimulate the market for a wide variety of cultural activities. This does not just mean increasing supply through subsidized provision (though this has a vital role to play). It means using education and the media to generate interest. The way in which sport has developed in the last century is instructive. A combination of accessibility to all, media coverage, glamorization, provision of facilities, education and judicious subsidy has transformed a succession of amateur pastimes into some of the most potent generators of wealth in society. Crucially this is demonstrable at the local as well as the global level: whether we are discussing the local golf club and horse show or the Olympic Games. There is no conflict between local sporting culture and that of interest across the world. Globalization stimulates local desire for participation. Local activity provides the base of talent and public enthusiasm on which global success is built. There is no particular reason why the same should not be true for culture. Indeed, for much of the time it is.

None the less the core of cultural activity cannot provide all the answers to economic prosperity and regeneration. Neither does sustainable culture necessarily make people happy or more politically satisfied. However, those involved in advocating greater attention to, and investment in, culture have needed to inflate its social and economic benefits in order to catch the ear of politicians and (where private money is the main source of support) businessmen. They have needed to do so because, in the second half of the twentieth century, the belief that investing in culture was a fundamental part of the delivery of a civilized community has become detached from the political willingness to match the aim with adequate resources. The same reservations have now spread to commercial sponsors, aware that the publicity which they regard as the by-product demanded by shareholders can be supplied better by connections with sport than with art.

Sporting culture and its place in contemporary Western society requires a book of its own and in this study there is only space to refer to its vitality and importance and then leave it to one side. None the less in terms of both governmental and private-sector financing it is increasingly in competition for funds with the rest of cultural life. This means that the arts and their associated sectors (film, radio, publishing, design, etc.) have to extend their reach into everyday life in order to catch attention. Both to exploit and to counter this trend policies are emerging which confuse popular with democratic, the culture of lifestyle with cultural expression, and the peculiarities of everyday life in different regions, nations and ethnic groupings with the fundamental building blocks of culture. It is a conundrum which even the most knowledgeable authorities on the subject, let alone governmental policy-makers, have difficulty unravelling.

The problems

Ask cultural organizations what is their biggest problem, their most debilitating challenge, for the foreseeable future and they will almost certainly say, raising money. There are exceptions. There are a few venerable German orchestras, like the Munich Philharmonic, where the question of money is something of an embarrassment. But from Hobart to Lerwick and from Hawaii to Hungary getting the show open and the staff employed makes the cultural administrator's job an unnecessarily stressful one. It requires ingenuity, thrift, and a talent for spending more time talking to funders than organizing the cultural activity.

Ask governments what the greatest problem is and they will almost never admit that it is money. To do so would be to give themselves the task of finding more. They cite inadequate cultural management, over-ambitious programming, inflated prices charged by artists (in reality the top 0.5 per cent earn superbly well, the rest earn below-average incomes for their training and experience), and the fact that because culture is about the creative imagination, there can never be enough raised from taxation to satisfy the continuous expansion that putting the imagination to work implies.

Both views are probably right in most countries. There is a lack of stability in cultural organizations which can undo in weeks what has taken decades to develop. While this is also true of most commercial enterprises, somehow the risks of trade are accepted where those to cultural institutions, many of which are the stewards of centuries of tradition and heritage, are less easily reconciled to financial ruin. Politicians see and use culture (in its widest definition) as the most important reason for national pride and identity. As such, it is also the foundation of many of their most bellicose positions. In these terms, most wars (hot, cold or trade) are justified to the people who have to fight them on grounds of cultural threat, whatever the real power and greed motives. But when defined in the narrow terms of the activity and institutions that come under the auspices of cultural ministries, there is little day-to-day interest. Indeed in the United States it appears that culture comes principally to the attention of the administration when it perceives trade barriers to its audiovisual industries or becomes embroiled in debates about the morality of contemporary art.

Governments are hindered by the lack of political status accorded to culture as it is defined within cultural ministries. Both lack of status and financial insecurity are symptoms not causes, however. The more intractable problems facing cultural policy have deeper roots, are more complex and especially hard to untangle for politicians who are in office for less than a decade and cultural managers faced with the business of annual budget shortfalls.

Culture is both the most personal and the most political of subjects. Individuals define differently the aspects of culture that are most important and exercise their cultural rights – the cultural extension of the human rights of free expression and assembly – in individual ways. For some, adherence to a religion is overriding and colours every aspect of appearance and outward behaviour. For some the nation-state is the focus of cultural self-belief, the nationalism that leads from a view of historical justice for the possession of their land to a perspective that encompasses anthems and flags, traditions of everything from eating times to jokes about other nations. For others the regional nation, with a separate language, style of dress, and often a traditional sense of grievance against more powerful (or just larger) neighbouring countries, is the driving force of cultural allegiance. And there are those who are less preoccupied with questions of territorial identity and define their culture through a more international passion for music, dance or the visual arts. Only the last, however, translates from a generalized attachment to the symbols of cultural identity into a willingness to treat cultural activity as an important part of everyday life and to expect provision to be made for it by government cultural ministers. For the rest culture is subsumed into more general areas of policy: planning legislation protecting the landscape and man-made heritage, the distribution of broadcasting licences, the provision of bi- or multilingual signs and forms, employment legislation respecting religious holidays or dress codes, national defence of territory and resistance to international regulations that harm traditional practices or interests.

In the broad category of culture governments need to be aware that these fiercely held convictions are increasingly in conflict with one another, not only within easily defined geographical areas but within communities. It is clear when demands for regional autonomy take on cultural colours, equally clear when a religious or racial minority becomes alienated by the apparent rejection of the host society. Dealing with such issues in a liberal and balanced fashion is far harder. Claims of territorial rights based on original occupation and cultural practice are throwing the legal systems and the tempers of both sides of the question into turmoil in Australia, the United States, Canada and New Zealand. Issues of language and education are more central to the divisions in Ireland than religion (though that is the symbol used in civil unrest). Recognition of regional differences based on the historical chronology of settlement, to which language (sometimes clearly separate, sometimes closely related), is leading to the political fragmentation of Europe just as it is seeming to unite at the governmental and monetary levels.

To list and examine the myriad regional grievances in Europe, let alone come to a conclusion about their rights and wrongs, would require far more space than I am afforded here. None the less until central governments have the policies to keep these divisions from becoming brutal, they may long regret their complacency. The behaviour of the communities in former Yugoslavia, goaded into action by the Serbian political and military élite fearful of losing power, is an extreme example, one hopes. But it would be foolish for other European governments to believe it could never happen to them. London and Madrid have both suffered half a century of bomb explosions because one small part of their nation-state has refused to accept its constitutional position. This refusal is based on cultural resistance as much as the desire for power over legislation and resources. Now the compromise between the cultures that created Belgium is at risk of coming apart and the tools being used to make it happen are language and education; passionate causes in a region where on the surface there is a common culture of religion, theatre, music and ethnic homogeneity. Austria is the latest country to have political turmoil fuelled by cultural antipathy. In a nation where there are far fewer reasons for disaffection than in almost any in the world, cultural mistrust is being used to justify an ideology of nationalist exclusivity. It is ironic that it is doing so just as one of the post-Yugoslav nations, Croatia, which emerged with just such an ideology, is now turning away from it towards a more inclusive and less alienated approach – though it will be many years before those with experience of the intimidation and bloodshed will feel secure.

Defining what are cultural rights for identifiable groups and what are unreasonable demands (based on a vindictive sense of grievance for injustice done to previous generations) is difficult for governments, particularly when the emotional appeal and the ease of mounting an opportunity for media attention lies so clearly with the complainants. In the United States recently some Indian nations have demanded that all human remains held in museums be reburied immediately in ancestral sites, because a skeleton was discovered in Washington State which appears to suggest that they were not the only 'native Americans'; there may have been immigration from Asia or Europe well before any previously suggested contact. Such a claim by either side has huge implications. 'White' scientific and cultural values come into direct conflict with the religious and political demands, expressed through cultural practice, of others. The chronology of settlement is indivisible from contemporary claims on property and resources, as well as political sympathy. Suggest through archaeology that the accepted version of ethnic migration is inaccurate and the historical edifice inherent in cultural self-portraiture essential to both European American and Indian American starts to come apart.

Both may be right in their own terms. Both cannot be accommodated. Effectively the Indian side is prepared to destroy permanently the archaeological record of its own people in order to secure short-term political advantage – the chance to make further claims for the restitution of land and the resources that go with it. Much the same argument is under way in Australia and, to a lesser extent, New Zealand. The rights of those whose ancestors settled the countries in the last three centuries are being challenged by the descendants of those who occupied, but did not necessarily possess or exploit, the land before their arrival. In anthropological terms it could be said to be a further chapter in the 7,000- year (at least) battle between farmers and hunter-gatherers. In political terms, if allied with the sort of regional and racial splits in Europe discussed above, the process could tip Western political systems either into repression or disintegration.

Culture has become a political weapon. It is highly effective. Appealing to a notion of group cultural rights carries an emotional charge and public-relations appeal which a bare claim to land and money would not. It exacerbates liberal guilt for previous exploitation. It allows activists to reinvent their culture, welding together elements that may have very disparate origins into a coherent vision – a process seen in all centuries and in most regions of the world, whether it be the Soviet and fascist systems of the 1930s or the rather more benign reinvention of Scottish Tartan culture in the 1820s by wealthy anglicized Scots who had spent the previous 300 years trying to stamp it out. With such an intractable problem we can perhaps forgive American politicians for not wanting to be offered the chance to create the post of Culture Secretary.

Stepping aside from the wider cultural context, there are problems, too, for governments in their stewardship of the core cultural activity – the arts. In terms of political philosophy they are being pulled in two ways at once. In one direction the arts are the highest achievement of civilization, the memorials that a successful society leaves behind as its contribution to posterity. This view includes the best of the architectural and plastic, the performing and literary arts. It takes a position that only the best will survive and that the art that has the highest chance of being regarded as the finest quality work, the most novel or intellectually sound, should receive the greatest financial support, even if it appeals in its own time to a relatively small proportion of the population.

The other direction leads to a view of culture where the designation of quality is based on popular success. The alternative is élitist: not élitist in the sense that only the élite in an art form should be championed (which attracts a measure of agreement from all) but élitist in the sense that only a self-appointed élite will be involved in appreciating the true quality of the art, freezing out the broad mass of the people from their temples. Therefore to be democratic, the reasoning goes, support should only be given where the arts can prove that they are making themselves accessible, are doing much of the thinking for the audience so that the public can respond whether or not they have had the education and the foresight to develop a set of informed critical values for themselves. This approach has the added attraction that governments looking for financial savings can retreat from providing systematic and extensive arts education for all and, when people complain that they don't understand, blame the arts for being obscure.

Those who work in the arts contribute to much that shows artistry but is mostly only entertainment. If no borders are drawn to the arts then they can include almost anything that passes the time skilfully and exhibits craftsmanship, from needlework to epic film. Artists are by their nature subversive, especially where the definitions and categories of others are concerned, and will produce plenty of work that is shallow, ephemeral and satirical, to the discomfort of both élitists and the proponents of populism. The purpose in these cases is to make the establishment look ridiculous, whether the establishment is a model of snobbery or of politically correct mass inclusion. To the latter, the arts become just an element in lifestyle culture, the creative research department of the design, advertising, broadcasting, decoration and catering industries.

When justifying their call for a significant political status, arts organizations will draw attention to exactly this contribution to wider social life and point out, too, as an economic corollary, that where there are artistic institutions, there tend to be better lit streets, more restaurants, tourists and a general sense of liveliness. Investing in the arts, they argue, is one of the few ways to keep a city centre from stagnation.

It is unsatisfactory, though, to define art as that which needs government or philanthropic finance to flourish. Commercial theatre, book publishing, television drama and the classical recording industry all survive (albeit with frequent failures) just as well as the subsidized sector. Many examples have become global phenomena and the dividing line between public and commercial art is unclear. For example John Caird's production of the stage musical version of Victor Hugo's *Les Misérables*, which has been franchised around the world, started out as a subsidized production for the Royal Shakespeare Company (RSC). Indeed the RSC would probably have collapsed by now had it not been able to rely on the global commercial income from the show. But where does government draw the line? Are some forms of music outside the definition of art? It is hard for government to say yes, especially when it is the forms that are least complicated artistically that have the largest popular following. Yet a minister who stands up and suggests that the veteran rock group Status Quo is as important an artistic phenomenon as the Berlin Philharmonic Orchestra (or the Beethoven it plays) risks being laughed out of office. The approach that 'everything is wonderful because it is a sincere expression' is both an evasion and a relegation of art to the psychiatrist's couch; an attractive but rather expensive form of personal therapy.

It is true, though, that in a democratic society, government spending has to meet the general approval of the taxpayer. Therefore winning the hearts and minds of voters is vital if public money is to be spent on the infrastructure and presentation of art, within the broader context of a vibrant and commercially successful culture. Because it clearly is possible for some artists and some forms of art to fetch very large sums of money, it becomes complicated to argue that financial gain is not the true measure of worth employed in the arts. Politicians do not like complicated issues, neither in general do they like activities the benefits of which will only be clear to posterity, long after they have left office.

None the less, it remains one of the justifications for government and philanthropic contributions to the arts that they offer an alternative definition of profit. Even if money is made in the process, it does not have to be the motivating force. The profit sought can be in less tangible but equally beneficial forms – greater self-confidence, less aggression, the stewardship of tradition, a more articulate and creative population are among the suggested advantages. Greatest of all is the profit of understanding. This cannot be predicted and is always elusive but it is the profitable quality which means that art is never only for art's sake, even if over-praise of the art's failed attempts to illuminate (perhaps 80 per cent of work produced) can appear depressingly decadent in their own time. Thankfully most of these will disappear into deserved oblivion, leaving the high-quality work to exhibit the predicted profit.

The benchmarks of artistic posterity and of licensed subversion, both paid for by a sceptical and often indifferent public, are not surprisingly difficult for governments to recognize. This is compounded by the fact that the arts in the West are in a period of unprecedented indiscipline. The confusion of styles, media, aesthetics and taste accurately reflects the explosion of choice in an affluent consumer society and the range of influences brought to bear on any mind. Where in the past an artist's points of reference were largely the sights and sounds of his or her own time and place, now television, recorded music, travel and the cheapness of books has meant that the points of reference are myriad – an artist can draw on any movement or style from the last 4,000 years and feed it through the filter of contemporary technology. If there is a critical label to be attached to this period (in succession to the Renaissance, the Age of Reason, Romanticism, Modernism, etc.), I would argue that we are now in the Age of Eclecticism. We select from a menu that is as long as we wish to make it. We can be as inclusive or narrow in our influences as we wish. There are no rules, no guides to good taste, no conventions that cannot be circumvented or just ignored. This makes critical judgement even more difficult than it has been before.

Artists are as free as their imagination and as well-informed as their Internet search engine allows them to be. We are free but, ironically, this brings skill and intention even more into critical focus than usual. Artists have no monopoly on wisdom and they will reflect the complete spectrum between stupidity and brilliance to be found in any profession. For the visual arts in particular, transfixed at the moment by the moment – transitory images and installations for which impermanence is inbuilt – the line between economical inspiration and perfect nonsense is very fine. At least in the past there were a few valid prejudices and academic rules to rebel against. The artist in the West now has true freedom of expression. But deciding whether that freedom has been well used is much harder; and in a democratic society where arts education for the majority is not exactly rigorous, the accusation that art is a waste of time, energy and money can only be refuted as an act of faith.

This does not tell the whole story though, for like commercial sponsors, while governments enjoy being associated with the established quality of the national heritage, they also want to be thought of as innovative, youthful, exciting and different from their dull predecessors. Even when art is at its most baffling, if it can be marketed as fresh and at the cutting edge, there is a public-relations advantage to be gained from being connected to it. However, governments, like large foundations, are never quite sure that they are not being made to look ridiculous. And so between themselves and the artistic practitioner they place layers of bureaucracy, panels, peer groups and councils designed to reassure sceptical finance ministers that public money is not being misspent.

The freedom of the artists in the West is only true as regards the content of the work. In all other aspects it is one of the most fussed over and supervised professions. A quite disproportionate amount of time is spent administering criteria for the distribution of, in government terms, very small amounts of money. The true waste is not in the arts themselves, it is in the administration of the arts. Paradoxically many of those working in arts administration are not doing so by choice. They are doing it because they want to be close to the work they love but cannot earn a stable income producing by themselves. A poet in the West is paid almost nothing for writing poetry. However, an income can be procured by teaching poetry, administering poetry competitions, writing about poetry, running workshops, giving readings, programming festivals and making radio shows. All of which – while valid and necessary to stimulate enthusiasm in the general population – presents huge obstacles to finding time for the contemplation and study that is necessary to write more good poetry. The problem is less acute for novelists and screenwriters (because the financial rewards are generally greater) but many composers, playwrights and painters are in the same frustrating position.

The generous system of flexible university fellowships and foundation-sponsored posts in the United States and (to a lesser extent) Canada goes some way to alleviating the situation. In Europe there is a remarkable network of residential centres for writing and creation which allow artists to live and work for a period without charge. This still does not recognize, though, that the only artists who can afford to take advantage of such opportunities are either those young enough to have no responsibilities or rich enough not to need the service. In the middle are those who have a home, family and bank loans to support, and for whom three months without pay is not an option.

While the funding institutions are worrying over the details of how every penny is spent on living culture, governments are failing to provide the one service to the general population that would justify the trouble they are taking. While they are building modern concert halls, refurbishing museums, subsidizing tickets, restricting damage to the heritage and almost starting a trade war over film quotas, they are failing to provide people with the basic critical faculties to become informed participants and audiences.

The education system in all Western countries is failing the culture. The teaching of history is unbalanced and often inaccurate. The teaching of the arts is inconsistent and too often regarded as play, not academically valid work. Arts organizations are increasingly expected to provide the educational environment that public education services have neither the money nor the training nor the instructions to offer to anything like the same standard expected in mathematics, languages or sport. This problem is not about the training of professionals in the arts and heritage conservation – more people are studying cultural subjects at tertiary level and seeking employment in the field than ever before. Rather it is about equipping those who are not in these professions to make use of them; to enjoy concerts, get into the habit of watching plays and reading poetry, visit art galleries and museums with an informed eye. It can also be argued that the human right to an education includes proper cultural preparation and therefore that governments that fail to provide it are culpable under the relevant conventions.

If they do fail in this regard education ministers are also undermining their government colleagues. As a result, culture ministers will be wasting the money they administer, promoting activity that will be decreasingly viable in terms of audiences and earning capacity (and democratic legitimacy) – a situation that is becoming rapidly evident in the United States. As was pointed out above, finance ministers will be deprived of the economic benefits of cultural expansion at a crucial moment of decline in manufacturing if sales of recorded music, books and admission tickets also diminish. The added value of cultural tourism will be lost if people only seek the sun and the bars. The rejuvenation prospects of city centres will be damaged if, unable to rely on the retail sector, they have nothing culturally interesting to offer. It will impoverish our civilization and render it capable of technological advance but without meaning or purpose beyond the purely commercial. The charge of élitism against culture – other than the culture of food, drink, sport, clothing and low-quality broadcasting – will be self-fulfilling. Then the budget stress that affects cultural organizations (and with which I began this section) will become acute as the interest of governments, sponsors and even philanthropists is diverted into other causes. They will do this because the 'golden glow' of public approval for cultural good work has been dissipated in a sea of disdain and indifference.

The requirements

'Good science', Arthur C. Clarke said recently, 'is just common sense worked out'. The same might be said for good cultural policy. Unfortunately common sense is not as common as we might like to think. For Western Europe, which has had overt cultural policy for eighty years and de facto policy for several hundred, it would be tempting to think that it already satisfied the conditions of the word 'sustainable'. North America is split between two diametrically opposed views of how to organize policy. In the United States it is assumed that the federal authorities have little or no say in cultural support. There are cultural industrial interests which it seeks to protect through trade negotiations. There is a small but constantly questioned role for the National Endowment for the Arts (NEA, which offers nothing like the proportion of budgetary support common elsewhere). There are entrepreneurial state arts commissions offering matching finance, some subsidy (the amounts varying enormously) and advising on the legislative framework – though they are not major features of all states – and there is the real cultural policy: the accumulation of the sets of criteria which govern the distribution of money by thousands of philanthropic foundations and the wide non-pedagogical role taken for the good of the community by many universities.

It is a haphazard and inefficient system, ensuring that most cities in the United States have magnificent new cultural buildings but a very limited social base for audiences and a relatively small number of viable cultural organizations in comparison with both the geographical and population size of the country. It also means that, compared with their counterparts in

France and Germany, US administrators spend a quite disproportionate amount of their time filling in application forms, making presentations to funders and pampering the egos of rich benefactors.

While there is a great deal of good work done – nobody can argue about the quality and energy of many American arts companies or the superb facilities for literature and performance in the universities – there is a sense that cultural life in the United States is inward looking; that there is little connection between groups – either from town to town, ethnic society to others with similar concerns, or out across the world. The American cultural sector, for all its conferences and bright publicity, does not network well and there is no organization, other than the weak and undermined NEA, charged with drawing the threads together from across the vast country. The voluntarily funded Public Broadcasting System distributes fine programmes but cannot match on its own the overall public service obligations placed on regulated broadcasters elsewhere.

However, the system does have its advantages. Despite occasional attempts at censorship by politicians (usually on grounds of public propriety and religious orthodoxy), organizations are largely free of bureaucratic interference. Their local supporters are fiercely loyal and generous. Cultural life operates in a climate of general respect and popular approval, even from people who do not actively participate in it. Those companies that do thrive, like the Metropolitan Opera or the Santa Fe Festival, do so to a level of financial solvency that their equivalents in Italy, the United Kingdom, the Netherlands and Australia can only dream of. Perhaps because of a nervousness that the interest of benefactors can only be held for so long and in the realization that state support will never fill the gap, many organizations have built up endowments, some of which are capable of guaranteeing their operating costs for several years ahead. While there is no such thing as permanent security (even massive endowments run out eventually if they are not constantly replenished), this offers a measure of insurance against short-term changes in fortune. It is an area that organizations in other regions should investigate seriously if they do not wish to continue being permanently at the mercy of political fashion.

Canada, which as ever faces towards the European and American systems simultaneously, has needed to reinforce its institutions over recent years as federal and provincial governments have veered between enthusiastic support for culture as the distinguishing factor of Canadian life and rhetorical support deprived of adequate funds (arguing that it is government's job to set the policy framework but not to pay for the results). The United Kingdom, Australia and New Zealand have followed much the same course, with political enthusiasm not always related to increases in central spending. Indeed in all countries local investment seems to be failing to keep up to a sustainable level. Meanwhile a great deal of government time and energy is spent on the reorganization of distribution mechanisms without evident benefits for the cultural sector itself.

Even in France, Germany and the other mainland European countries, while the tradition of up to 90 per cent reliance on public money has been retained for major institutions, others (such as festivals and touring performing companies) have seen either a lessening of support or increases failing to keep pace with need, so that the proportion of state aid to outside earnings has changed markedly. Another dimension to European cultural policy and support looked set to be added to the equation when, in the Treaty of Maastricht, the European Union (EU) legitimized cultural spending by the European Commission for the first time. However, the conditions attached, particularly that requiring unanimous agreement by all member states and a co-decision procedure between the Council of Ministers and the European Parliament, have effectively frozen activity to the level at which it was when the Maastricht Treaty was being negotiated, even after the revisions of the subsequent Treaty of Amsterdam. With several countries jealous of their national role in cultural affairs, and Germany's regional governments equally jealous of allowing the federal authorities to have any role in cultural discussion with the EU, paralysis looks set to continue for many years to come. Disappointingly, the EU, which could become a major force in cultural reconciliation and artistic internationalism, is being left instead to treat culture as a flag-waving exercise and occasional project co-ordinator.

This gives the general background to the requirements in cultural policy in the countries that, despite their geographic distance from one another, are being treated here as one region of the world. This is partly by virtue of their relative wealth but also because of similar attitudes to non-political control of cultural expression, similar proportions of public money allocated to cultural activity (where most use substantial direct funding and some minor fiscal concessions, the United States does the reverse but the net result in terms of gross domestic product is much the same) and because of the relative maturity of their cultural management systems.

There are perhaps five conditions for policy if it is to be sustainable; sustainable not just in financial terms but in human rights, environmental and developmental terms as well. There needs to be political balance, realistic investment, a socially liberal legislative framework, encouragement for cultural enterprise and industry, and enlightened education. In each country and on each continent this set of conditions will translate into different measures and mechanisms. However, in the main the policies themselves should be comparable and should have similar goals.

Political balance in culture is important if the culture is not to become the plaything of extremist interests, as it has in Serbia and the other countries of former Yugoslavia. Balance involves promoting culture for its own sake rather than the political objectives of any particular party or dogmatic philosophy, especially aggressive nationalism. It is hard for nations to realize, because they have so much at stake, that almost no citizen exactly fits the model of the perfect national. Dig back one or two generations and almost everybody will have strong family or residential connections with somewhere else. Therefore the promotion of a national culture must be neither the sort of commercial exploitation which turns a country into a jolly heritage theme park, constantly harking back to a golden age of cultural purity that never existed, nor so monothematic in its view of what it includes that the vision of the culture is false and, in the worst sense, exclusive. The successful culture is one which is open to all (whether or not they have an ethnic or nationalistic reason for being interested), is self-confident enough to include variations and opposing arguments, and vibrant enough to believe that the culture of the present is just as interesting as that of the past.

There must be balance, too, in the policies that determine the extent of human rights in relation to culture. A determination needs to be made that rights of expression lie with the individual, not with a group who can cite their collective will as being more important that those of the individual. If these rights of expression include the right to use any chosen language, to produce, exhibit and distribute cultural work, to be fairly considered for available cultural funding programmes, to travel and study for cultural purposes and to be able to publish work in any form, regardless of whether others are offended. Rights based on the individual mean that everybody has a right both to offend and be offended, to publish and either refute or ignore the offending material. These rights also impose a duty of self-restraint on powerful authorities not to impose their own cultural prejudices on those around them or to impose on culture their social preoccupations.

Keeping connected and involved with the results of cultural support while maintaining an arms-length detachment from the content and programme is often recognized as an objective by governmental authorities but very seldom achieved. It requires cultural ministers not only to insert a bureaucracy with peer-group assessment into the decision-making process but also to stand back and abstain from the manipulation of the bureaucracy to reflect the precise thinking of the government. To set policy, support it with money from taxation, accept the ultimate accountability for the results of legislation and spending, and promote the wellbeing of culture all without interfering (even when provoked) is a difficult task. The creative results, however, will prove a significant asset for the country. This does not mean that governments cannot act as patrons, commission work for diplomatic and state purposes, aim to involve the population widely or use culture as a major tool in their programmes. They both can, always have done and always should. Where governments at any level must stop and stand aside is at the point where they claim that culture, rather like God, is on their side; that they have a monopoly on and somehow can claim ownership of the culture – that it is in their service. Stepping back while maintaining enthusiasm and interest will always lead to the most sustainable policy.

The system will require constant interference and crisis management, however, unless cultural activity is backed with sufficient resources. Most Western governments, with a wide variety of channelling arrangements, devote between 0.4 and 2 per cent of their total annual spending to culture. The lower limit means that the need for money dominates almost every conversation between the cultural sector and government, a wearying experience for both. The upper percentage is generous and should produce highly effective work. But it needs to be carefully managed, with a significant proportion earmarked for new and expanding initiatives if inflated, stagnant organizations are not to tie up more than the share of the money that can be used productively.

The most effective policy is one where direct grants account for around 50–60 per cent of the required institutional annual operating budget and other incentives are put in place. Money-raising should not obliterate the management's working day but at the same time needs to offer a substantial enough target to prevent complacency. The incentive measures can include contributions to endowment funds, donations out of lottery proceeds, individual and foundation donor schemes (with tax allowances), sponsorship packages which can encompass an element of challenge funding from the public purse, the proceeds of galas and merchandising and bonuses for reaching sales or participation targets.

A broadcasting regime that uses a high proportion of artistic talent and itself invests directly in performance and the literary arts is these days essential. I would propose a new financing initiative, too; one that tackles the problem that the arts are cross-border in character but taxation systems are not. An international fiscal agreement making donations via the Internet to cultural organizations around the world tax deductible at home would be a visionary new way to support the international health of culture.

One of the biggest handicaps to maintaining effective cultural policy in many countries has been the professional status accorded to government employees working in cultural ministries. Too few have training or expertise in the subjects with which they deal. Culture is not like social security or defence. It has to deal with an emotional context and a fragile and unpredictable set of organizations. The cultural sector is changing constantly and an adequate knowledge of it cannot be learned in a few weeks of reading briefing documents. Too often cultural operators are faced with officials who do not understand the sector or government's unusual relationship with it. This is not helped by the fact that the culture ministry is often seen as a professional cul-de-sac, attracting only those who are being moved down or sideways from departments that carry more political weight. This is something governments can address simply and quickly. They can train cultural officials specifically for the task. They can move people regarded as 'high flyers' in the profession to cultural ministries and they can ensure that officials make a proper career in cultural service instead of moving out of it almost as fast as they moved in.

The effect of low esteem in cultural departments can be felt throughout the public service. Politicians themselves treat culture as a bit of a disappointment. If the quality of policy is to improve then becoming culture minister, being appointed to the parliamentary culture committee or being handed the cultural brief in a foreign or trade ministry must be seen as an enviable promotion, not a step towards political oblivion with the compensation of a few free tickets to the opera and to football matches. If the quality, dedication and professional confidence of officials is low it will translate into inadequate legislation and missed opportunities for cultural contribution to other areas of responsibility. Having cultural expertise can be a liability in the education system as well. Very few music or art teachers are ever made head teacher. Increasingly the posts go to those with science, mathematics or language (in its technical rather than cultural guise) backgrounds.

Low status has also hampered attempts to integrate cultural considerations into other areas of government responsibility. It is crucial, however, for the successful delivery of a coherent cultural programme that the implications in all areas of policy are properly recognized. Sustainability will not be achieved unless this is implicit. There is a cultural element in almost all ministerial briefs; obviously in education and diplomacy but no less inventively in rural and environmental affairs, health, economic development and even defence. Conversely, policy in departments such as employment, trade and social benefits can have important but often unintended consequences for cultural activity. There is an essential need to bear in mind both the opportunities and the effects when taking executive and policy decisions throughout the system and for drawing up effective strategies for using culture in economic and social planning.

The legislative framework in virtually all Western countries contains most of the basic requirements for freedom of expression, cultural investment and education, though the opportunities are not always pursued as vigorously as they could be. In particular the fiscal systems, both for taxation and social benefits, rarely recognize the different working patterns and career structures of those working in the cultural sector from those working in commerce or bureaucratic posts. Ireland, the Netherlands and Finland offer some interesting examples of how imaginative restructuring of regulations can stimulate the cultural contribution to the social and economic fabric. But even in these countries the process has required a great deal of lobbying and has been undertaken with considerable political reluctance at first. Countries need to take steps to co-ordinate their fiscal and benefit systems to give maximum encouragement. This is not just a matter of offering tax concessions and generous unemployment pay. Indeed most cultural sector workers do not want to be seen as the beneficiaries of state charity. But it is possible to draw together the way tax is paid, the requirements for eligibility to social payments (recognizing, for example, that artistic work in progress is work even if it is not being paid for in advance), copyright, pensions and contract law.

The work permit and visa systems need to recognize the international and free moving nature of cultural work. Too often visiting performers, teachers and creative artists are treated as though they are economic migrants or undesirable aliens. In a recent example a very well-established Russian pianist, resident in the United Kingdom, was beaten up by German immigration agents when he arrived to fulfil a concert engagement. Despite the ensuing diplomatic embarrassment, no serious action was taken to make sure such incidents do not happen again. This small-mindedness only serves to make the officials that perpetrate it look historically ridiculous, no different from those of Tsarist Russia and Metternich's Austria who kept Tchaikovsky and Chopin waiting at border posts (though even they did not assault the composers). It is an attitude that should have long disappeared. The music belongs to everybody.

Just as the taxation system should cater for the unusual nature of cultural activity so should trade legislation. Cultural artefacts and texts cannot be treated as no more than manufactured goods and corporate services. Ideas and the media through which they are expressed need to circulate freely, while being protected against piracy. The ownership and conservation of objects that are valuable to the heritage of a particular country or group needs to be protected, while allowing for viewing, loan and exhibition as widely as possible. Despite the popularity and profitability of the auction houses, there should be: restrictions on the markets allowing objects to be traced and conserved; a duty placed on collectors to exhibit (much as owners of great houses in receipt of grants have to open them to the public); and provisions that allow artists and their descendants a share of the sale price when the work is resold or reproduced.

Broadcasting and film (and their ancillary industries) also have a cultural component which has to be balanced with their industrial value. The preservation and spread of language, the geographical distribution of talent, the development of different aesthetic values and dramatic traditions, and the continuance of technical skills all necessitate policy towards production and distribution which allows public financial support, whatever the strict commercial interests of the free market. Cultural integrity should always be allowable in international legislation governing trading relationships as a reason for protective intervention.

In the long term, however, all the policies of encouragement, protection and fair reward will be in vain if all the people are not offered broad, deep and lifelong opportunities for cultural education. All children should be aware of, and have participated in, the main elements of cultural life by the time they leave school. The opportunity to play music, write creatively, discover drama and the visual arts should be a part of every school week. History should be taught in a balanced and coherent way, neither ignoring the personalities and chronology of the past for the history of lifestyle, nor offering only the history of victorious societies as important. There are many great cultures which the violence and accidents of history have treated unkindly but which offer lessons, values and ideas of continuing worth. After leaving school, people should have the chance to deepen their knowledge at any time, either by re-entering formal education or by taking up the offers of cultural organizations. By the same token no cultural institution in receipt of public money should operate without a programme of liaison and development with the education system. In societies where knowledge is no longer passed on by oral repetition, where cultural reference is essential for social inclusion, and where the speed of change makes it all too easy to become disorientated, the excellence of education is one of the few ways government has of equipping its citizens for the future.

Summary digest of requirements for policy-makers

POLITICAL BALANCE

Enshrine the rights of the individual before the group. By taking the individual as the holder of cultural rights, policy-makers put the competing demands of ethnic, regional and special interest activists in a more manageable perspective.

Divorce cultural expression from territorial claims. Recognizing flags, songs, languages, 'pressure group' assemblies, dress, food, sporting allegiance and distinctive art forms is all part of laudable diversity. Translating that into territory, unless there is already an identifiable and viable territorial unit, is to encourage a concept of nationhood that could destroy present political structures. There is an argument for scrapping the nation-state system, regrouping smaller autonomous countries within much larger regional alliances, but the world order may not be ready for it yet.

Promote diversity. By defining successful nations in terms of the rich variety of cultures they contain, rather than projecting a homogenous image of one 'theme-park' national culture, countries will be better able to limit the appeal of separatist movements.

Cater for minority languages, especially through broadcasting. Until recently broadcasting channels were a comparatively rare resource. Digital broadcasting means there is no reason why any dialect or minority language cannot be accommodated and encouraged without alienating majority-language speakers. There is equally no reason why mainstream broadcasting stations cannot offer 'opt-out' facilities for small but important language groups, as the BBC does for Gaelic in Scotland.

Ensure history is taught even-handedly (there is no group, race or country that has behaved perfectly). Children love to know who won. The answer should avoid the concept of final victory, especially where there has been great suffering in the process. It should be explained that states have been born painfully but that only telling the victor's story is not the whole truth, nor does it accurately reflect ethnic and cultural reality. Equally, instilling the idea that one group are eternal victims can be damaging, as it psychologically justifies compensatory aggressive nationalism (as among the Hutu, and in Serbia, Ulster and Israel). None of us are genetically quite who we think we are and a concept of belonging can be more important in peaceful modern society than the facts of ancestry and settlement.

Resist the temptation to ban or censor, except on the grounds of incitement to hatred or violence. There is no reason why people should not be challenged or offended by what they see, hear and read. They have the option to ignore it. No religion or culture should be allowed to impose its social dogma on others (or even on its own followers if they choose to reject it). However, to encourage people to hate or to commit violence is to allow them to attempt to remove the rights of others and cannot be permitted.

Present national culture positively, not as being better than or opposed to others. This is normal policy but there are still a few states that define themselves by what they are against, rather than what they can offer. It is this attitude that usually leads to unrest and bloodshed.

Strengthen international networking and projects. The intercultural community is larger and more active than rigid governmental and funding systems, limited by borders, can accommodate. Finding ways to link people together through their professional lives is the most effective way of promoting understanding and providing a reservoir of people who can combat mistrust.

Make access and conservation the key criteria for heritage policies rather than ownership. In reality legal possession should no longer be the deciding factor governing the ability of the public to see and conserve the heritage. A thousand years ago in Europe all property was in theory held in trust by individuals for the community (via the feudal state). There can be a modern equivalent by which ownership confers a duty of stewardship in return for the enjoyment of possession and exploitation. The stewardship should entail the duty to preserve and, within a balanced regime of the right to privacy, to make the protected heritage available to others. This principle should apply to landscape, archaeological remains, buildings, objects and documents. Governments should put in place tax systems (for example, exemption from property taxes) which make stewardship not only possible but attractive to owners.

Have in place an independent arbitration system (sometimes multinational) for political disputes with a cultural basis. Culture provokes emotional defence like almost no other aspect of human affairs. It will often take the calm and patient eye of an impartial observer to see the means of reconciliation.

Recognize the cultural implications in all other policies. This is already part of the EU Treaty of Amsterdam's article on culture. It is a sensible injunction, allowing governments to realize that environmental, economic, trade and fiscal policies, among others, are all just as likely to impinge on culture as those specifically designed for it.

Enhance the professional status of public cultural officials and politicians. Culture will not enjoy good policy or be able to withstand pressure from other areas of interest if those who are meant to promote and implement policy are regarded as second rank.

Have in place a form of independent advice on the distribution of funds. Removing accusations of bias or political motivation from funding decisions is essential if cultural organizations are to remain impartial in their public dealings and stable after changes of government. Do not then seek to manipulate or undermine the independence of the advice.

Publish advice and, if it is rejected, provide the reasons why. Transparency is the fastest way to remove mistrust. If decisions are made in the open they can be challenged but will carry a legitimacy that secrecy will always undermine.

Develop research and information tools. Without a strong and accessible base of evidence, it is as difficult to run sustainable cultural policy as it is to manage the budget or improve the environment.

BUDGET

Be prepared to devote to culture at least 1 per cent of central public spending, with a higher proportion by city and rural authorities. Countries continue to define the elements included in cultural spending in different ways. In this context it does not much matter whether spending is defined as actual money granted or taxation foregone through concessions. With such a diffuse area and such different delivery systems, this is inevitable. However, if the core aspects of institutional support and enterprise incentives are included, the 1 per cent called for by the European Parliament more than twenty years ago is fair. Several countries spend twice that anyway, others a mean half that or less. Because culture is a larger part of local government responsibility than of central's, it is inevitable that a sustainable infrastructure will require a higher proportion of spending at that level.

Expect to support cultural institutions to 60 per cent of operating costs. While this may vary a few per cent in either direction, a balance needs to be struck between the ability of the institution to fulfil its basic remit and its wish to innovate and experiment. A completely funded organization which never has to worry about money can often become dull and complacent. On the other hand one that is always on the brink of collapse will not be able to provide the service, quality or the range of activities for which it was founded.

Support organizations, not only projects. Bureaucracies often find it easier for their own annual accounting systems to support projects that are finite and costed rather than the continuing expenses of running an organization. However, too much emphasis on project finance can distract an organization from its central work, while leaving it without the administrative structure to sustain activity. In general cultural organizations prefer the reverse arrangement to governments: coverage of their office and personnel costs with matching funding available for projects.

Make donating attractive to business, foundations and individuals through fiscal incentives. Altruistic philanthropy is usually an indulgence only of the very rich. For the rest of business and the middle-income population, which cultural organizations need to tap if they are to raise significant sums from the private sector, there needs to be a persuasive gain as well as a tradition of giving.

Encourage long-term endowments to make activity more self-supporting. Endowments have the advantage of shielding organizations from political fashion while making them seem less spendthrift to citizens. They also offer an appeal that feels to the donor more like an investment in the future than spending in the present.

Never expect culture to make money. If it does, reward accounting procedures that reinvest profits (do not lower the following year's level of public finance). Deficit financing always makes organizations look inefficient and forces them to seem to be begging for money rather than offering a long-term service. The interest of the public, not the profit of the shareholders, needs to be seen as the motivational force. This does not mean that profitable cultural enterprises should be discouraged. Rather that there should be a wider definition of sustainability which recognizes that profit in terms of employment, social confidence and artistic achievement is as valuable as profit in money.

Expect every department of government to have a cultural budget. It is hard to think of a department that does not touch culture. Formal recognition of the fact can make policy more imaginative and help cross-government liaison.

Decentralize spending decisions but place on subsidiary authorities a duty to provide cultural infrastructure. Like many services culture is best decided upon as close as possible to the point of delivery. However, it is often too simple for local authorities to highlight other priorities that play on the insecurities of voters. Enforceable powers need to be in place to ensure that culture does not end up at the end of the list.

Draw up strategies for using culture in economic, social and environmental planning. Culture can make a clean, inexpensive and popular contribution. It will also carry more status if it is seen to be making a difference in other important areas of responsibility. However, culture cannot be the only answer to a problem. It should be seen as a vital but complementary factor.

Have a fund for new initiatives separate from that for continuing institutions. It is often easy to strangle new projects because all available funds are tied up in existing ones. For a culture to live there must always be room for fresh ideas to be taken up and nurtured.

Increase the funds for multinational organizations and initiatives. National authorities are traditionally bilateral in their approach to international projects. This fails to recognize the fast evolving nature of much cultural work, which can spin across borders as easily as air travel or the Internet. Yet the international funding system is, for the most part, stuck in the 1950s. Within the EU, member states are either suspicious that their own powers are being usurped or regard the culture budget as one through which they can demonstrate a puritanical approach to spending. In North America and Australasia international work is seen as carrying only limited domestic appeal. In all cases this is a myopic viewpoint.

'Ring-fence' finance for core arts activity from that for initiatives with other policy objectives (education, diplomacy, social cohesion etc.). The opposite to including culture in all policy areas (referred to above) also needs attention. If the culture is not supported for its own sake, rather than that of other objectives, it becomes only an instrument. Culture needs to follow its own instincts to develop.

Support the research and development side of cultural industries and the enterprise that fuels them. They will be vital areas of the national economy in years to come and, like defence industries during the Cold War, need public investment in order to serve the public interest.

Improve arrangements for the preservation, collection and lending of books, the archiving of electronic media (audio and visual) and access to it, both physically and digitally. At the moment we enjoy unprecedented access to the culture of the past but it is easily dispersed and erased.

LEGISLATIVE FRAMEWORK
Separate benefits to self-employed (or occasionally employed) cultural workers from unemployment regulations for other sectors.

The cultural sector (especially the arts, crafts and audiovisual areas) contains a higher proportion of self-employed people than almost any other. This lifestyle often involves long periods without formal contracts or periods when creative work is being prepared but has not been paid for. Few benefit and welfare systems take account of these unusual circumstances, treating culture as the same as any other service industry. This wastes talent, reduces enterprise (forcing people into unsuitable work when they could be doing something more useful in their own field), increases the debt of those who borrow to avoid the benefit system, and wastes the time of welfare agencies dealing with a mismatch between procedures and reality. The Netherlands has recently devised a new mechanism which goes some, though not all, of the way to improving the relationship.

Support copyright and other intellectual property rights through new international tracking and collective payment procedures. The Internet and digital broadcasting have revolutionized the way material is distributed. While mechanisms for gathering dues need to be reformed, the new advances only constitute novel forms of publishing and should be treated as such. They do not supersede the framework for rights built up over the last century.

Regulate the tax regime to allow for maximum voluntary contributions to cultural organizations. Treasury authorities should learn to view such contributions as a policy target, not as a suspicious form of tax avoidance.

Require high-quality cultural content on all publicly regulated broadcasting media. Forcing the quality of public broadcasting down-market by making it dependent on advertising not only makes it an unfair competitor with genuine commercial channels, it reduces the quality level of the broadcasting culture. High-quality content on public channels will, in contrast, raise the quality of commercial channels by association.

Produce environmental and cultural protection legislation that is complementary and strengthens both. The concept of the cultural environment is emerging because both sectors share so much of the same ideals, jargon and intellectual background. Protecting the environment will almost always protect culture. The reverse is not always true but when it is, culture can be an effective ally in delivering policy.

Conclude an international agreement on the definition and extent of cultural rights. Such rights have begun to be perceived as being a secondary extension of basic human rights. However, insufficient work has been done to distinguish and identify them. Yet many of today's political minority issues can only be tackled once the legal landscape for cultural rights is brought into focus.

Review and liberalize travel, employment and visa requirements for those involved in cultural activity. Artists and cultural communicators pose no threat to foreign governments. They are traditionally mobile and yet are perhaps more devoted to their own locale than most other professionals. Gaining the experience of living and working among others for a time is the way to spread understanding. The immigration rules should be adapted to reflect this.

Secure international agreement on the movement of cultural goods and services . . . balancing the need for free trade with the rights to cultural access of citizens and the integrity of the cultural context and environment.

Enshrine in law the principle of political non-interference in artistic content. This both protects politicians from accusations of attempted censorship of free speech and from pressure to intervene, and protects artistic practitioners from tyranny. The legislation should also seek to prevent governments directing their arms-length agencies in matters of artistic judgement, though not in laying down criteria for high-quality work.

Vigorous legal protection for archaeological sites should be enacted. This would include arrangements for the replanning of building and agriculture to preserve and display sites in context. Such legislation should override other, more transitory cultural interests (e.g. religious belief) or economic reasons (expense).

INDUSTRIAL SUPPORT
Incorporate cultural aspects into all public development tenders, regeneration plans, training programmes and lending agreements. This has two effects. It increases the local provision of cultural facilities without extra cost to the public purse, and forces those dealing with the plans to be more aware of cultural responsibilities. Once again there are corollaries with emerging environmental practice.

Require public and private development plans over $250,000 (at 2000 prices) to prove cultural benefit. This is an extension of the previous condition. It increases clearly the contribution to community development.

Allow interests of cultural diversity to override free-trade arguments in commercial legislation. This will be controversial with free-market economists; it is essential if national attempts to protect smaller languages and less commercial forms of expression through investing in their recording and distribution are to succeed.

Exempt support for cultural industries from restrictions on subsidies. The maintenance of cultural identity is more important than the purity of the market.

Bring together, through tax concessions, cultural industries, artistic organizations and training institutions. While those who work in culture move naturally throughout their careers between the industrial, the public and the non-profit sectors, those sectors themselves are often too separate for their own good: book publishers from festivals, for example, or film distributors from drama schools.

EDUCATION
Ensure cultural subjects are given high status in all parts of the education system. It has become too easy for arts subjects to be treated as non-academic, recreational or non-vocational. As a result too few arts teachers receive promotion; the faculty of arts and humanities becomes devalued; the artistic and other cultural humanities become unnecessarily separated.

Insist on arts subjects as part of the compulsory curriculum at all levels (high school and university courses should be widened if necessary). If they continue to be regarded as optional, then large sections of the population will fail to gain the knowledge on which to build their interests in later life.

Make the cultural context and environment a specific area of study. There is too little research on how the environment and culture interact and how the cultural characteristics of society are formed. Policy would be on a far firmer footing if universities and NGOs were encouraged to investigate and communicate the results.

Require all cultural enterprises in receipt of public money to have and to implement an education programme. Such a programme not only has clear benefits in terms of access for citizens, it also deepens the experience and widens the outlook of those working in cultural organizations.

Provide facilities and encouragement for life-long cultural education. School learning is not enough, especially since many people develop their interest in and appreciation of culture later in life.

Enable all children to participate in cultural activity. Just as in football the subtleties of the game are learnt by playing, not by copying down the players' positions from a blackboard, so active learning through participation is the only effective way to bring cultural subjects alive. And it is in participation that professional artists can best help in the school environment.

Make it a duty of government to ensure all children leave school prepared to make the most of the cultural opportunities and facilities around them.

12,13